Cope With
Bereavement

Aileen Milne

Edited by Denise Robertson

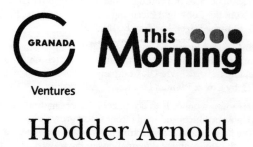

Ventures

Hodder Arnold

A MEMBER OF THE HODDER HEADLINE GROUP

Orders: Please contact Bookpoint Ltd, 130 Milton Park, Abingdon, Oxon OX14 4SB. Telephone: +44 (0) 1235 827720. Fax: +44 (0) 1235 400454. Lines are open 09.00 to 5.00, Monday to Saturday, with a 24-hour message answering service. You can also order through our website www.hoddereducation.co.uk.

British Library Cataloguing in Publication Data
A catalogue record for this title is available from the British Library.

ISBN-13: 978 0 340 94317 5

First published   2007
Impression number 10 9 8 7 6 5 4 3 2 1
Year   2012 2011 2010 2009 2008 2007

Typeset by Transet Limited, Coventry, England.
Printed in Great Britain for Hodder Education, a division of Hodder Headline, an Hachette Livre UK Company, 338 Euston Road, London, NW1 3BH, by Cox & Wyman Ltd, Reading, Berkshire.

Hodder Headline's policy is to use papers that are natural, renewable and recyclable products and made from wood grown in sustainable forests. The logging and manufacturing processes are expected to conform to the environmental regulations of the country of origin.

Aileen Milne (BA Hons. Dip. Couns. MBACP and author of *Teach Yourself Counselling* and other publications) has been a counsellor for 14 years and has worked in many different settings. These have included counselling at a Young People's Counselling service, running counselling related and Assertiveness Training workshops for local authorities and as part of a team that took counselling into local schools. She has worked with a broad spectrum of people's problems, including the painful effects of bereavement. She currently writes, works for an Employee Assistance Provider and counsels privately.

Denise Robertson's television career began with *BBC Breakfast Time* in 1984. She has been the resident agony aunt of ITV's *This Morning* for the last 20 years. In that time she has received over 200,000 letters covering a wide range of problems from viewers and from readers of her newspaper and magazine columns. She has written 19 novels and several works of non-fiction. Her autobiography, *Agony: Don't Get Me Started,* was published in paperback by Little Books in July 2007. She is associated with many charities, among them Relate, The Bubble Foundation, Careline and the National Council for the Divorced and Separated.

WHICH PAGE?

My heartfelt thanks to all the people who have shared their stories with me, as their counsellor, at their time of loss. I feel privileged for having been part of their healing process.

I would also like to dedicate this book to all the dearly loved people in my own life who have died.

Aileen Milne, 2007

The stories within this book represent those presented in bereavement counselling, they are not verbatim accounts – confidentiality has been upheld.

CONTENTS

Part 2: Taking Control – The Next Steps 85

FOREWORD

By Fern Britton and Phillip Schofield

As presenters of ITV's *This Morning* over many years we have met many incredible people with many incredible stories to tell. What we have learnt is that life can be wonderful but it can also be very hard.

Our phone-ins have generated thousands of calls a day from viewers all over Great Britain looking for suitable advice on a range of subjects. What is very obvious from these calls is that we are not alone with the personal challenges we often face and there is a great need for help in dealing with them. We are always cheered by the follow-up letters and emails from viewers saying how our experts' advice has helped them to turn their lives around.

Over the 20 years *This Morning* has been on air, Denise Robertson, our agony aunt, has regularly offered support and advice to millions of viewers on a huge range of personal problems and she spends even more time off-screen answering letters, calling those in distress and dealing with questions via the internet. As a result she is uniquely qualified to edit these books which reflect the common sense and sensitive advice that we provide on the show.

We believe these survival guides will help you to deal with the practical and emotional fallout caused by issues such as bereavement, relationship break-ups, debt, infertility, addiction, domestic violence and depression.

If you feel that your particular problems are insurmountable – don't! There is always a way to improve your life or at least get yourself on a path towards a new start. If you think you are alone with your problem – don't! Our experience shows that many of us face the same problems but are often reluctant to admit it. You have already made a great start by picking up this book.

We both wish you all the strength and support you need to tackle your own personal problems and sincerely hope that we can help through these books and through our continued work on the programme.

INTRODUCTION

I have had to face the loss of loved ones too many times in my life. The first time, when my father died, I thought the pain of grief would kill me. I would learn that even the worst grief eases with time and you find yourself able to go on again but the death of my first husband affected me badly. I had depended on him completely so I lost not only a lover and a friend but also the person who had carried me through life. I had to 'grow up' very quickly because I had a child to support. I suppressed my grief and carried on but I paid a heavy price for that suppression. Now I know that grieving is a natural process and an important one. It needs time to take its course if you are to heal.

No two people are alike. Some grieve openly and their misery is written on their face. Others cover up their feelings and they smile and chatter or maintain an icy calm. They are not unfeeling, they are simply managing as best they can in their own way. And sometimes loss can make you behave, for a while, in odd, even bizarre ways so that you ask yourself 'Am I going mad?' Those who mourn are not the only people who have to deal with loss. We can all feel at a loss when faced with bereavement. How many times have you seen someone you know to be grieving and thought 'I don't know what to say'? The bereaved write and tell me of old friends who pretended not to see them when they passed in the street and it reminds me of the anguished eyes of my friends as they have sought for the right words at sad times and of my own occasional inadequacy when confronted by unbearable grief.

All death is tragic, even after a long and well-lived life, but some deaths are tinged with extra pain – the loss of a child, or a death by suicide that leaves a host of questions that seem to have no answers. Also, whatever the circumstances, there are many practical things that must be dealt with, at a time when you probably feel less capable than you have ever felt before. This book is designed to help with those practical questions and with your sadness, too. Above all its intention is to reassure you that what you are feeling is normal and that one day your world will cease to rock upon its foundations and you will find peace. Believe that the people involved in the book want to understand and help. I hope it brings you comfort.

Denise Robertson

Part 1:
What to Do
Right Now

In Part 1 we look at how you might expect to be affected by grief in the early days and weeks of bereavement. First, we outline how you might feel and behave and how your body might respond at this traumatic time; we then move on to guidance on practical matters before looking at where and how you might find emotional comfort and support. It is our intention to offer comfort, support and advice throughout.

The first few days

If you have been recently bereaved our hearts go out to you. Bereavement can be one of the most difficult of human experiences and in the first stage of bereavement you are likely to be going through many different emotions and you might feel confused about what you are thinking and feeling. What you must remember is that whatever you are feeling is understandable and it is okay to feel and behave differently from how you might in normal circumstances. Try to accept your feelings and not fight them. Some feelings might be unfamiliar and out of character for you but you are responding in a way that is right for you at this moment in time. There are no rights or wrongs about grieving. Also try to remember that there is help available and you needn't go through this alone.

Where you are right now, where you will be soon

After the death of a loved one you are most likely to have some symptoms of shock. This can happen even when the death is expected. When death is sudden, shock is likely to be accompanied by denial, 'This couldn't have happened – you've got it wrong.' Shock affects us in many ways. You might feel that your world has been turned upside down and you don't know how you are going to cope. For some people it feels as if the world they knew has stopped and they can't understand how everything and everybody seems to carry on as normal.

Some people are (temporarily) immobilized by grief, unable to think clearly or speak with anyone. You might be unable to put into words how you feel, you perhaps need to lean heavily on others, or feel that you need to be strong for others. You might believe that the person who has died is around, that you feel their presence. You wouldn't be alone in thinking this. Many people talk of their deceased loved ones being with them at times in their lives and especially in the first days and weeks following the death.

Some of us find relief in crying, while others aren't able to cry at all. Perhaps you are unable to do much – you feel as if all the energy has drained from your body. You could feel agitated and unable to settle at anything. There might even be an outburst of laughter that can come with shock.

Other common symptoms of the first stage of grieving, when you are likely to feel numb and shocked include:

- Slow or incoherent speech.

- Talking quickly and incessantly.

- Slow or quick movement.

- Heaviness in the limbs.

- Hanging on to things for support.

If this happens to you, all it means is that your body and mind have closed down a bit to protect you from the initial strong grief emotions. Remember, responses like these will pass and are:

- Natural.

- Normal.

- Understandable.

It might be hard to believe at the moment that you will ever be able to get through this, but gradually things will change. Soon you will feel differently. If you are in dreadful heart aching turmoil right now, **be assured that this will pass**. Hard as it is to imagine now, gradually your life will return to a kind of normality. Later, you are still likely to grieve, because grief doesn't suddenly go away, but the grief will become more manageable. This takes time, so try to be patient with yourself. Your loss will still be painful but you will become more in touch with your emotions, and you will find the strength to carry on.

When I first heard of my son's death, I went completely numb. I could hardly move or speak. People kept asking me, 'Are you alright?' and I couldn't answer them – it was as if they were a million miles away.

Ellie

Coping with visitors

In the first days and weeks following the death you might have a lot of visitors – people calling round to check that you're okay and seeing if you need help of any kind. Their presence can be a comfort, but it might also feel too much at times. Flowers might arrive and it can seem like the doorbell is constantly ringing. Don't feel that you need to do it all yourself – delegate. People can take turns in answering the door, responding to phone calls, cards and letters. Interacting with lots of people can be exhausting and you might have to call a halt at some point. It might be a help if you restrict visits to certain times of the day, perhaps in the afternoons. If it all gets too much, take to your bedroom and rest. Make it clear when you or others need time to yourselves and try not to feel bad about it. It is important to look after yourself at this stressful time.

What you need to do right now – practicalities

Following a death, there are things that need to be done. These include informing friends and relatives of the death, collecting your loved one's belongings from where they died, and preparing a funeral. In some ways these jobs, as difficult as they are, give us something to do. People sometimes speak of keeping busy as the only thing that kept them together. For other people any task is too much in the early days, and in this case, whenever possible, it is best to let others take over. If this happens to you, don't be afraid to let people know you need help.

Letting people know

It is important to let people who have shared the person's life know about the death as soon as possible. The person might have left an address book, which will be helpful for contacting their friends and associates. In the early stages, all you need to do is call or send a simple written message informing friends and family of the death, saying that you will contact them again when the funeral has been arranged.

In the first days, you are likely to receive letters and cards of condolence. It can be a huge comfort to know that people are thinking about you. You might like to send a brief reply (or ask someone close to do this on your behalf), but don't feel that you need to acknowledge them straight away. Perhaps you will find comfort in replying to cards and letters at a later stage, when the funeral is over, but you don't have to respond to condolence letters if it feels too much.

People need to be notified again once the funeral arrangements have been made. Letters, telephone calls and an announcement in a local newspaper are all ways of doing this. A simple notification of the death and details of the funeral and family wishes is all that is required in the newspaper announcement. For instance:

Smith – On 20 October, Jane Susan Smith, dearly loved wife of Henry and mother of Karen and Edward, died at Clancy Hospital, aged 52. Funeral service at Greyfriars Crematorium, Northbridge on 24 October at 10 a.m.

The announcement can also include other requests such as: 'Family flowers only' or 'No flowers please', 'Donations can be made to…' and other details like 'You are welcome to join the family at Elms Lodge in Priory St. for refreshments after the funeral'.

Collecting your loved one's belongings

It can be so difficult to accept the reality of the passing of someone you love, and yet at this early stage of bereavement there are practical matters to take care of such as registering the death and picking up the person's belongings. If they died in a hospital a nurse will explain to you where you can collect the person's possessions (this is usually a hospital bereavement office). There are likely to be personal articles like clothes, books, a purse or wallet and jewellery to pick up. Collecting the belongings can be a wretchedly sad experience. If you have to do this job then take someone sensitive with you if you can.

If your loved one died in a nursing home, then they might have more possessions to collect, perhaps photos and ornaments as well as clothes. Talking with the nursing staff could be a source of comfort if they knew the deceased well. When the family are unsure about the deceased's wishes for funeral arrangements and disposal of their bodies, they might find it helpful to broach the subject with a member of staff who your relative particularly liked and who they might have confided in. It wouldn't do any harm to make a few discreet inquiries about any last wishes.

My mother had dementia for a few years before she died and the staff who nursed her in the nursing home were lovely to her. There was one nurse in particular who had a bond with Mum and I talked with her a lot when Mum passed away and she was a great source of comfort to me.

Lynn

Registering the death

A death is required by law to be registered at the local registrar's office within five working days. At the time of death, a doctor will have signed a death certificate, stating the cause of death. If there is to be an inquest into the cause of death, a temporary death certificate will be issued until this has been established. When the person who died is to be cremated a second certificate is required (Forms B & C & F), signed by two doctors. You, or someone else, will need to take the certificate(s) to the registrar who will then issue you with a green form to give to the funeral director so that the funeral can take place. If you don't feel able to cope with doing this or any other task at the moment, then try to accept how you are feeling and ask another member of the family, or partner, to take over.

Q: Is it true that we should only speak well of those who have passed away?

A: It's important to see the person as having been a full human being with human traits – with both positive and negative sides to their character. While it's best not to be unkind about the person, it's okay to be realistic.

Arranging and organizing the funeral

How to book a funeral director

In the first days of bereavement you will need to choose a funeral director. It is an important and necessary step but you might feel unsure which company to choose. Perhaps you know someone who has used a funeral director's firm in the past. Ask them if they would recommend them. Another way to find a funeral director is to look through Yellow Pages with a friend or other members of the family, whose judgement you value, and call round different companies and ask them about the service they provide. Alternatively, you could look on the internet for local companies. Funeral directors will come to your house to discuss your needs and requests as part of their service.

Funeral directors and their employees are used to being with those who are suffering a loss. As you would expect, they normally provide a sensitive, respectful service. Over the years they have added many facilities to their services so if there is anything that you would like them to do, then ask. However, be aware of costs and don't let anyone pressure you in any way. Small companies may offer a more personal service. It might seem mean or in bad taste to think about cutting the cost of a funeral but most people who have given it some thought, say that they don't want a lot to be spent on their funeral when their time comes.

Of course, it is possible for a family to do most of the pre-funeral arrangements themselves, with minimum input from the funeral director. The body can be washed and prepared by close members of the family or a partner and be kept at home for the period of a wake. Funeral directors are usually open to providing selected, rather than all, of their services and offering advice to the family. Some families, for instance, buy the coffin directly from the suppliers but might look to the funeral director to provide a hearse, cars and coffin bearers.

Obviously these matters need some thought and might be mostly suited to situations where death is anticipated and there is time to plan, but it's also worth remembering that, as long as a body is kept in a suitable environment and in good condition, then the funeral need not take place for up to a few weeks.

Here are some of the services funeral directors can provide:

- A choice of service sheets – they can arrange for these to be printed.

- The transportation of the loved one's body.

- A room for the loved one's body in a chapel of rest.

- Attendance at the funeral – hearses and coffin bearers.

- Burial or cremation services.

- A choice of caskets.

- A recommendation of a local stonemason (who will be familiar with the local church and cemetery requirements) for headstones, plaques and other types of memorials.

- Suggestions (and arrangements if required) for local caterers and venues for post-funeral gatherings.

- A breakdown of funeral costs.

Green and woodland burials

The person who died might have talked about a green or woodland burial. If no instructions were left, and it is up to the family to decide, you might consider a green or woodland burial and a more personalized type of funeral service.

Increasingly, funeral directors list green and woodland burials among their services. If the person was concerned about the environment in life, then a green type burial might seem appropriate. There are many woodland burial sites in the UK that are run by wildlife charities, private trusts and local authorities. The woods – created by planting young trees over the settled burial plots – provide a natural habitat for birds and wildlife. Woodland burial sites are in quiet, peaceful and secluded rural areas.

Companies that offer green services encourage families and friends to organize and take part in funerals, if they choose. If you would like more information about alternatives to conventional funerals you could look at *The Natural Death Handbook* or the Natural Death Centre website: **www.naturaldeath.org.uk**.

If you would like to have your loved one buried in the grounds of your home, then it is not impossible, but you would need to adhere strictly to government guidelines; for example, UK public health regulations require a grave to be at least 12 m (40 ft) from a watercourse, such as a mains water supply, and you would need the permission of the Home office.

How to arrange the service

Things to think about for the service include:

- Service sheets – containing order of service, music/hymns, poems and readings.

- Placing a notice in local papers to notify people of the death.

- Ringing or writing to friends and family members, colleagues etc. to tell them about funeral arrangements.

- Keeping the funeral director up to date with your and your family's wishes.

- Liaising with the minister or other person who will conduct the service.

- Asking people if they would like to contribute to the service.

You and other family members can choose hymns, music and order of service together. If there is any conflict about this try to let it go. You are all under stress and remember that, basically, you all have the deceased's best interests at heart.

Perhaps you and others would like to contribute to the service by reading a poem, telling a story about the person's life or saying what they meant to you. However, don't feel pressured in any way into doing anything you are not sure about. You might feel strongly that you want to make a contribution as a mark of the love and respect you hold for the person, but remember, you are likely to be feeling extra sensitive on the day and it might be enough to take a back seat in the proceedings. It might be enough for you if you think your own loving thoughts about the deceased during the service instead.

It is not uncommon for people to think ahead to the kind of funeral service they would like and leave instructions with their loved ones. Prior to death they might have discussed with those they trust, how and where they would like their bodies to be disposed of when their time comes. However, not everyone is comfortable doing this, no matter how much they love their families.

Having input from family and friends can make the service more personal and special, but if a duty minister conducts the service it might, inevitably, be less personal and it might be worth keeping this in mind. Whether the service takes place in a church, chapel, crematoria or in a woodland setting, we all want it to be a warm, meaningful 'send off ' for the person who died and a 'good' funeral can also be a real source of comfort for the mourners. To achieve this, the funeral content needn't be complicated but may just need some thought. We might ask ourselves what was special to the person, what did they like or value in life? For instance, you might like to choose a piece of music, that was enjoyed by the deceased or that relates to the person in some way, to be played in the church, chapel or crematorium.

You might choose to get together with family and friends to make arrangements for the funeral service or decide to do this yourself with perhaps the help of one other person, like your spouse, and with the guidance of the minister or person who is to conduct the service. Perhaps the deceased left their own instructions or guidelines for a service – this is not unusual.

These days, the funeral director and the crematorium staff are happy for the bereaved family to play a part in organizing and participating in the funeral. Often friends and family decorate the crematorium or church or other service room with flowers and toys (for instance, in the case of a child's death), or drape sports shirts or military flags or other emblems of hobbies, clubs and associations over the coffin. Photographs of the deceased can also be put on display.

Commonly, people will offer readings or poems, reminiscences, anecdotes and music (sometimes a member of the family or a friend will sing a favourite song).

Q: Will a funeral director transport a body from one part of the UK to another, for instance, England to Scotland, for a funeral?

A: Yes, funeral directors can transport the body of a loved one to another part of the UK. They can liaise with another funeral director firm in another location who can then take over with the funeral arrangements when the deceased arrives.

The funeral gathering

Usually the mourners get together for a gathering after the funeral. You might decide to have this at home or alternatively at another venue, which might be at a hotel or other function room where refreshments can be provided. If you don't know a suitable place then your funeral director will be able to advise you, or alternatively you, or someone else, could look in Yellow Pages and make enquiries.

If you decide to have the gathering at your home, then remember that there will be refreshments like sandwiches, cakes and drinks to provide, which will involve extra shopping, preparation and cleaning. It will mean more work and it might cause extra stress that you could probably do without. On the other hand, if you feel that you would like to do this and want to keep busy, you might find being at home more comfortable and congenial.

You are likely to meet up with members of the family and friends that you haven't seen for a long time. There might be people present who you have a history with or who are estranged from the family. Try not to get too embroiled in family politics should any arise. Let it all wash over you and remember why you are all there. Don't feel that you have to take the lead and be a host. Let people come to you and if you get upset while people are around then that is fine and understandable. People won't expect you to be on top form.

Perhaps you have decided that you don't want a get-together, for whatever reason, and that is fine too. Or, you might decide that you are not up to attending the gathering yourself, or that you want to leave after a short time – all of which really is okay. People will understand. Please don't feel pressured into doing anything you aren't comfortable with – you can always contact people later when you are feeling stronger.

Q: I'd like to have my father's favourite (blues) song played at his service in the crematorium. Is this okay?

A: Crematoria and churches can play recorded music. Various types of popular music are played at services these days.

What about religion?

If the deceased person is Christian, Muslim, Jewish or of another religion, the rituals, traditions and services will be the ones for their faith. (Please note that here the term 'minister' is used as a generic term for a religious leader and includes a Rabbi, Cleric, Iman, Priest, etc. The same applies to the use of 'church' to represent other religious houses like synagogue, mosque or temple.)

What do you do if the person has no chosen religion and has left no instruction for a funeral service? A religious service might not feel right. You could arrange a service that you would like to give them – something that reflects their character, interests, and the love and respect you have for them. A *Humanist* service can provide an alternative to a religious service. (Humanism is a philosophy concerned with human matters rather than religion). Sometimes humanist funeral services are held in a Quaker meeting house. You or a family member might like to contact the British Humanist Association (BHA) to find a local 'officiant' who can conduct a non-religious based service (*see* page 327).

If the deceased has said that they wanted a service in a church but they were not churchgoers, you will need to talk with the vicar or minister of the local church about planning the funeral. The funeral directors can find a minister for you and arrange a time and place for the funeral and they will talk you through all the other parts of the service. They (or another person who will conduct the service) can visit you at home to discuss your wishes and to hear about the person who has died so that they can personalize the service. They are likely to note down a potted history of the person's life and ask things such as when and where they were born, where they went to school, the names of close family members, spouse, children and favourite pets, where they lived, worked, and any interests they may have had.

Q: What is embalming?

A: Embalming (often now termed 'temporary preservation') keeps the body from decaying. It lasts for about three weeks. A chemical called formaldehyde is pumped around the body and injected into the abdomen. If you or others want to view the body, your funeral director will recommend that it is embalmed.

Legal matters

There are legal matters that will need attending to after a death. All you, or a member of your family, might need to do at this point, is to tell the firm of solicitors of the deceased's death. If the deceased has made a will, the solicitor will let you know about any developments and about any steps you might need to take.

The will

A will makes legally sure that the contents of our estate (our homes and possessions) are divided according to our wishes after we have died. The estate meets the cost of:

- Any outstanding tax.
- Debts.
- Funeral expenses.

Inheritance tax (IHT) may need to be paid depending on the wealth of the estate. (See the UK government website for tax and benefits: **www.direct.gov.uk/Inheritance.**)

The estate is managed by the person appointed in the will (the executor). If there is no will and executor, letters of administration are needed. You will need to contact the local probate registry – part of the High Courts of Justice – to access application forms. When you get written confirmation (authority to manage the estate) from the courts, you become the administrator of the will.

When everything has been paid, then the executor or administrator can start to share out what is left of the estate according to the will, if there was one. This might involve applying for probate – the proving of the will.

When the sum of the estate is quite small (currently about £5,000 or under) you don't have to apply for probate. The job of probate is to:

- Protect the interests of any surviving dependants.

- Make sure that creditors are paid.

- Assure that the estate is distributed in accordance with the deceased's wishes.

If there isn't a will, the next of kin will inherit the estate in the following order:

- A surviving spouse.
- Children of the deceased – or grandchildren if there is no surviving child.
- A parent of the deceased.
- A relative of the deceased.

If someone can show that the deceased was supporting them financially just before their death, they can claim a *share* of the estate.

When no living relatives can be found or any beneficiaries, then in the UK the whole of the estate goes to the Crown. For more information you can look at the Desktop Lawyer website: **www.desktoplawyer.freeserve.net/law**. It gives free legal information.

Telling other organizations

Although they can usually wait until after the funeral and aren't really important in the first days or week, you will need to tell other authorities about the death and deal with the deceased's documentation, including:

- Order books and giro-cheques from social security that will need to be returned to source.

- National Insurance papers.

- Car documents – driving licence and insurance (some of the fee may be refundable).

- Memberships to clubs, gyms and associations (some of the fee may be refundable).

- Library books.

- Loaned equipment such as oxygen machines or wheelchairs.

- A child or young person's school or college.

- Employers.

- Any life insurance policy the deceased had.

- The Inland Revenue.

- The Benefits Agency (if any benefits were being claimed).

- The post office (to re-direct mail for a time).

- The council or housing association (if the house the person lived in was a council or association property).

- Electricity, gas and telephone suppliers.

MYTH: It is always better for the dying person to have someone they love with them when they die.

FACT: It is not something we can know for sure. It has to be remembered that people are slipping in and out of consciousness when they are near to death.

2

Emotional lifelines

We have looked at some of the practical issues you might face in the early stage of bereavement. Sometimes we are kept so busy at this time that we hardly notice how we are feeling. Yet it is important that you do pay attention to how you are feeling and make sure you are looking after yourself in any way you can. So, with this in mind, let's look at what you might be feeling and how you can best deal with your thoughts and feelings.

What you might feel right now

Someone precious to you has died and you are deeply affected by the loss. You might feel differently from how you expected. You might feel overwhelmed by emotion or you might feel too stunned to cry. Perhaps you were with the person at their bedside when they died or maybe you heard of their death over the telephone. You might have rushed to be with them or this might not have been possible – they may have died in another country, far from home. Whatever the circumstances, you are likely to feel deeply affected by the death. You might find it hard to believe that the person who has played a significant part in your life has gone. It might feel impossible to take in.

At the moment you might feel that you don't know where you are. Your emotions could be all over the place – perhaps you are feeling anxious, even traumatized. You might be saying to yourself, 'Can this really have happened?' Everything can feel unreal. You might feel helpless. Perhaps you can't do anything but sit and cry, or pace the floor. Perhaps you feel guilty, maybe telling yourself, 'I could have done more', and 'If only I had been there with him.' Maybe you blame others. Some people say things like 'The doctor didn't listen', or 'The emergency services should have got there quicker.'

Remember, these thoughts are completely normal. They are your way of reacting to your terrible feelings of loss. Maybe you are trying to find reasons for the death to make it more manageable, as it is making no sense. Thoughts like these are part of normal grieving. Right now you might feel that you will never feel good about life again, that the bottom has dropped out of your world. You might be asking yourself 'How can I live without this person in my life?' Platitudes offered by others who care such as 'Time is a great healer' or 'He's in a better place', may seem cold comfort at the moment. Others mean well, and might need to comfort you, but they don't always say the right thing (or perhaps it just doesn't feel like the right thing).

MYTH: I could have prevented the death.

FACT: It's very unlikely that you could have done anything to prevent the death. Guilt is a natural and normal response to bereavement, particularly sudden bereavement.

Understanding what happens to us, when we grieve, in our thoughts, emotions and behaviour can help us immensely.

Here is a list of things that are quite normal to feel after a loss. Do you recognize any?

- Sadness.

- Anxiety and helplessness.

- Guilt.

- Numbness/detachment.

- Exhaustion.

- Anger.

- Shock.

- Depression.

- Relief.

If you feel all or most of these, don't worry, you are not going mad. They are normal reactions. They won't last; they are completely understandable given the circumstances. In time your emotions will settle.

Remember this:

Accept what you feel and let it run its course. You will be fine – you will get through it. Take things day by day, moment by moment and step by step. If you find yourself suddenly crying or laughing uncontrollably, take it as a sign of release and not as a bad thing. Above all, **be kind to yourself**.

MYTH: I should be strong for others.

FACT: You are coping as best you can at the moment. It is important that you let your emotions out if you need to. Your body is responding naturally to stress. You might be able to give comfort to others at times, but it is important that you look after yourself.

Q: A very close friend of mine died in a car accident recently. I can't get over it. I go over and over things in my head. Am I going mad?

A: No, you are not going mad. You are grieving the loss of your dear friend and are trying to work things through in your head (that is, make sense of what has happened) and this is a normal response.

The first few days and weeks after the death

Your emotions

Sadness It is normal to feel sad when you are grief-stricken. Some say that feelings of sadness are there from the beginning, that straight away there is a sense of missing the deceased person. Sadness can come over you quite suddenly.

Anxiety and helplessness You could feel helpless, anxious and insecure. Maybe you are thinking, 'What will happen in the future – how will I manage?' If you are an older person this can be very real. As a woman whose husband has died you might think, 'What if I die too – who would look after the children?' A solicitor will help you to appoint a guardian for this unlikely event.

Guilt Often we feel guilty about things we imagine that we could or should have done to alleviate the person's suffering. There can be guilt that we were not able to protect our loved one. There can be feelings of 'I should have been there when they died' or 'I could have been kinder to them.'

I was racked with guilt after my dad's death. My mother told me that it was my fault he'd had the heart attack – that I'd worried him to death. On a rational level I didn't really believe it, but deeper down I did, because we had a difficult relationship.

Dan

Numbness, detachment Perhaps you are unable to feel or show emotion around the death of someone close to you. You might feel an icy calm come over you. You could feel stunned – as if your brain has gone into a state of stasis. In our grief, we can withdraw emotionally.

Exhaustion Lots of things can make you feel exhausted. Perhaps you are not sleeping well. Maybe you are anxious and worried about the future. If you lose your appetite, smoke more cigarettes, or drink more alcohol than usual, you are likely to feel the effects. Anxious and panicky thoughts can add to the exhaustion.

Anger This is commonly an outlet for pent up feelings that are difficult to manage. When we feel angry we don't have to grieve. The target for our anger can be someone else, for example, a doctor or nurse who is believed to have been negligent; we can target the anger at ourselves or at the person who has died, and left us behind. In the case of suicide, there can be feelings of, 'How could he do this to me? How could he cause so much pain?'

Shock You are likely to experience shock early in bereavement. Perhaps you feel disbelief. This can happen to you even when death has followed a prolonged or terminal illness and even when you have expected the person to die.

Depression Many of the symptoms we have in our early grieving are similar to the symptoms of depression, such as poor appetite, sleeping problems, feeling tired, poor concentration and no enthusiasm for living. You are unlikely to be clinically depressed in the early stages of grief. You might have temporary *reactive* depression, which means that you have a reason to be depressed.

Relief We might experience relief when the person dies, for example, when they have been ill for some time and suffered in their illness, we perhaps feel relief that their suffering has come to an end. We can feel relief for both them and ourselves, because it is hard for us too, to watch those we care about suffer. However, feelings of relief are sometimes accompanied by guilt.

Remember, feelings like these will pass. Try to accept them and let them run their course. Tell yourself these are normal responses to losing a loved one and that you will get through it. Don't expect too much of yourself at this difficult time.

Suicidal thoughts

Sometimes people see no sense in carrying on without the loved one in their lives. You might have had thoughts about killing yourself, or had fantasies about joining the person who has died. You might feel the pain is too hard to bear.

Perhaps if you are older you have had a lifetime with this person and don't feel like carrying on. However, given time and support you can rebuild your life.

If you are having suicidal thoughts then please see your doctor straight away. If it is happening to another person urge them to do the same. You could also ring a crisis helpline like the *Samaritans* (*see* page 331) or a friend or family member who would understand.

Mood swings

Mood swings are quite normal. You are likely to feel calm some of the time and feel as if you are going crazy with grief at other times. You are likely to be more irritable with other people and yourself at this time. It can all feel more than you are able to endure and you want to know if things will ever be less painful. They will. Again and again we will be telling you that time is the principal healer. **Trust in the healing effects of the passing of time and your own abilities to recover and heal.**

Finding help, love and support

There is no way you can avoid the pain of the experience, but you don't have to go through it alone. There are lots of places to find support and hopefully you will be offered the kindness of friends, family and the community where you live. If you live alone, have limited contact with social networks and feel cut off from others, get in touch with a relative who might be able to support you, or talk with a neighbour. Try to be with people whose wisdom and judgement you trust. The local religious community, the funeral directors or a doctor could also support you or give advice.

Remember – in these first days and weeks it is completely normal to:

- Have mood swings.

- Feel panicky.

- Feel jumpy.

- Be more clumsy than usual.

- Feel irritable.

- Feel really intense emotional pain.

- Need the support of others.

How your body reacts

You might not be paying attention to how you are feeling physically – there is so much going on emotionally. Try to keep tabs on your physical state. You could be breathing more quickly and shallowly than you normally do due to stress, so start by taking some slow, deep breaths when you are able. Be careful not to breathe too fast or you might hyperventilate. To relax your breathing, breathe in slowly to a count of four then breathe out to a count of six. Tell yourself that you will get through this and you will. Heavy sighing is a sign that your oxygen levels are low and you are trying to breath in lots of air at once to compensate. For similar reasons you could be yawning a lot. You might be tired and exhausted and your body is running on adrenaline.

You might notice that your concentration is poor. Your batteries are likely to be running on low – as if all your energies are going into grieving. Loss of concentration can lead to losing things and having little accidents. You might be prone to clumsiness, forgetfulness and absentmindedness. You might be preoccupied with thoughts of the deceased and the circumstances of the death.

Sometimes people report that they feel

physical sensations like tightness in their throat or chest, or they feel sick, weak or light headed. Breathing deeply but slowly will help and so will making an effort to relax your body (*see* Part 5, Chapter 16). Begin by sitting or lying down quietly for a moment and noting where you hold tension in your body, for example, for some it may be in the stomach and for others the shoulders. Then let the tension drop away by relaxing that area of your body. Try to look after yourself – give yourself extra care.

Q: What agencies can I turn to for counselling and advice?

A: The *Citizen's Advice Bureau* can help with advice on practical matters; the *Samaritans* is a 24-hour service that provides someone to talk to at the end of the telephone, and *Cruse* provides a bereavement care service (see Part 5, Chapter 18).

Sleeping and your dreams

It might be hard at the moment to get regular sleep. If you are not sleeping well at night, then try to nap in the day. When you are newly grieving (and for many for some time after) it is normal not to sleep for many hours at a time or find it hard to get to sleep or you might wake very early. It is also really common to dream about your loved one, alive and well. Of course waking up to a different reality can be devastatingly hard.

By dreaming about the deceased your mind is trying to come to terms with the situation; you have lost someone close to you, and you might be struggling to accept the enormity of what has happened. Our dreams might be happy or sad – we might find ourselves crying or talking to the person in our dreams. Whatever the dream is about, one element is common to the content – we are trying, as best we can, to work through our grief even as we sleep.

Some people might want to sleep more and there is nothing wrong with that. Our bodies heal themselves during sleep and you might need more rest than usual at this time. So it might suit you to go to bed earlier and sleep a little later and take naps throughout the day.

Eating properly

Don't be surprised or too worried if in the first days, your appetite goes. Of course, longer term it is important to your health that you eat well but it won't do you any harm to miss a few days of substantial amounts of food. Try to eat something if you can, to stop you feeling light headed. Soup is a great standby and of course tea and coffee can be a comfort but mind your intake because the caffeine could add to any edginess you feel. A milky drink at bedtime would be a good idea as well as a long, warm soak in the bath.

Relatives and friends might suggest that you have a stiff drink but watch your alcohol intake. In the very short term it might seem to help but clouding your emotions won't be helpful longer term. Similarly, if you smoke, try not to increase your smoking, because again this might have negative consequences on your general well-being. Remember, you need to look after yourself.

MYTH: You need to eat to keep your strength up.

FACT: It won't do you any harm not to eat much for the first few days. Eating heavy meals when you're upset can make you feel worse than not eating.

Physical signs of bereavement can include:

- Shallow breathing.

- Sighing and yawning.

- Tightness in parts of the body like the throat, tummy and chest.

- Aches and pains.

- Weakness in the muscles of your body.

- Loss of appetite.

- Tiredness or exhaustion due to lack of sleep and stress.

My friend died after an overdose.
I hardly ate anything for a week.
I drank loads of tea and coffee with
friends and had a drink and smoked
endless fags but I kept going, like I was
functioning on pure adrenaline.

Mark

My sister died in a very traumatic way.
I lost my purse, fell down in the street
and forgot where I had left my car, all
in the first week following her death.
I drifted around the house leaving cups
of tea everywhere – I was totally
preoccupied.

Ruth

3

Your grief, your feelings, your friends and family

We all react differently to death

How we cope with the death of a loved one can depend on the way in which they died and how close we were to them. Every death is different. Some deaths might need more making sense of. For example, the death of an infant or child is usually harder to cope with than the death of an older person who has lived a full life and died a natural death. It is always devastating for a parent to outlive their child. It doesn't seem to tally with the natural order of life.

Try to remember that everyone is different and that it is not always easy to predict how a person will react to a death. If you are a middle-aged man, who has lived with your mother all your life, you are likely to take the death of your elderly mother badly even when she has had a good life and lived to an old age.

Close friends and family and more distant contacts

There will be some mourners who haven't had such a significant role in the deceased person's life as the main mourners. These people are perhaps in more of a position to support those more heavily affected by the death. Main mourners are direct family and close friends; other mourners might include more distant family members, colleagues, teachers and neighbours. Sometimes not all the main mourners are identifiable – a close childhood friend for example.

I felt on the edge of the mourners. I wasn't recognized as a main mourner but, when my lifetime friend Julia died, I felt devastated. Fortunately, I was able to ring Julia's family and tell them how I felt and was invited to meet up with the family. This helped me enormously.

Becky

Those around you might have strong responses to the bereavement. They might feel guilt or anxiety and think things like, 'I should have helped the deceased more' or 'My son is the same age as Tom was when he died, perhaps he too could die of leukaemia.' Perhaps, like you, they feel very upset and under stress. Some people might not know what to say to you, and, although you would like to see them, they stay away and you feel hurt by what seems like their lack of concern. However, it is likely that they don't stay away out of unkindness. It might be because they don't know what to say and they are afraid they might hurt you further by saying the wrong thing or they feel that anything they say will be inadequate. Give them the benefit of the doubt – maybe they will come up trumps at a later stage.

Q: Flowers are welcomed, but I'm not sure if I should send a funeral wreath to the family house, to the church or the funeral directors?

A: It's probably best to send sprays or wreaths of flowers to the funeral director who will take them to the place of service. If in doubt you could check with the family or call the funeral director directly.

It helps to talk

One thing we do know is that when we are recently bereaved we need to talk about those who have died, and it is really important to feel listened to. It helps tremendously when we can talk, sometimes over and over again about the deceased; what they were like, what they enjoyed in their life. Sometimes we need to talk about how much they suffered in illness. People tend to flock protectively around the recently bereaved. Friends and members of our families will often send cards or letters or make visits to give us their condolences and offer love, advice and support. Their presence is very reassuring. Their concern can make us feel less alone with our strong emotions.

Visitors might ask us questions like, 'Where did the person die?' or 'Where were you at the time they died?' Answering questions like these can help make the loss seem more real for us. Talking about the deceased's character or exploits can also be comforting at a later stage (this might be done for the first time at the post-funeral gathering), but usually in the first period of bereavement it is the circumstances of the death and how we are feeling that is usually the focus of conversations.

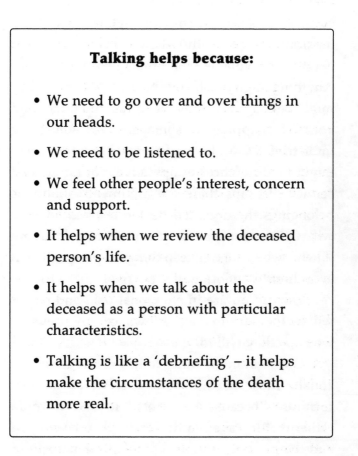

Talking helps because:

- We need to go over and over things in our heads.

- We need to be listened to.

- We feel other people's interest, concern and support.

- It helps when we review the deceased person's life.

- It helps when we talk about the deceased as a person with particular characteristics.

- Talking is like a 'debriefing' – it helps make the circumstances of the death more real.

How to cope when things get tense

People generally want to comfort each other, but because emotions are running high there might be tensions between the mourners. If you feel emotionally volatile then others probably do too. Anything might push your buttons. Sibling rivalry might be exaggerated by the upset. You might find yourself snapping at someone over something quite trivial. Couples might end up arguing. There might be differences of opinion about the funeral service. Perhaps there are arguments about the belongings the deceased person left behind, or a will. Other people's behaviour can be hurtful but it helps when we can keep things in perspective. It is a highly emotionally charged time for all concerned. You are in emotional pain and others will be too – try to make allowances for others, as we hope they will for us.

One man in his fifties talked about giving his cousin most of a deceased relatives antique furniture, 'because he wanted it, and I would rather that it stayed in the family than be sold off and the proceeds shared.' While his generosity is admirable, it is perhaps wise to resist being impulsive, making quick decisions and regretting them later.

Two sisters from a close-knit family found themselves arguing because one told the other that she intended taking a well stocked pile of toilet rolls from the deceased person's house. This practical idea infuriated the other woman. She took it as a sign that the other person didn't care about the deceased.

It can be the most insignificant little things that set people off but this is likely to just be a release of strong pent up feelings. Let yourself laugh if it comes naturally. You are still allowed a sense of humour. It might seem inappropriate to laugh when you are mourning, but it isn't. Laughing, like crying, provides an outlet for pent up tensions and the deceased wouldn't grudge you a few moments of light heartedness.

Remember:

- It is a difficult, trying time for everyone – be tolerant and keep your cool.

- Tensions may make your buttons easy to push.

- We feel more vulnerable and are more easily hurt when we are newly bereaved.

- Others may behave strangely (think of the toilet rolls!).

- Try to be tolerant.

- Keep a sense of humour.

Let others help

Try to communicate your needs to people who want to help and let them. You might usually be an independent sort of person who isn't used to asking for or receiving much help. But now is the time. There are many practical ways that neighbours and friends can be put to good use; with picking children up from school, driving you around if need be, or walking the dog. Some of the more onerous formalities around death, for example, registering the death, can be shared with other members of the family. If you are an only child then a partner can help. If you haven't got a partner then friends can be called on to go with you as support. Neighbours or friends might be kind enough to provide meals. Liaising with funeral directors and religious ministers, or those responsible for conducting a ceremony, can also provide much needed reassurance. Your local social services are another source of advice.

Getting help from your GP

You might wonder if you would benefit from some medication to help you cope with some of the feelings following a loss. There is ongoing debate about whether it is useful or not for us to take anti-anxiety or antidepressant medication or sleeping tablets when we show signs of overwhelming stress and can't sleep. While some people swear by the benefits of taking medication for a short time, others are strongly against the idea. If you are worried about your health and are feeling depressed or unable to cope it is definitely a good idea to seek the advice of your doctor and talk over your options.

Reasons for and against taking medication

For:

- Antidepressants aren't habit forming.

- Some people find them helpful in dealing with their grief.

- Medication can help in cases of depression and prolonged grieving.

- Sleeping tablets can help you return to better sleep patterns.

- Your doctor has given it their consideration and is advising you to take the medication.

Against:

- Antidepressants can take time to work – up to eight weeks.

- Sometimes they don't work.

- Different drugs might need to be tried before the right one is found.

- Some doctors think that taking medication can interfere with the grieving process.

- Sleeping tablets can make you feel groggy in the daytime.

4

Where to look for comfort and reassurance

We need to look after ourselves while we are grieving. Hopefully you will have a lot of support and comfort from others, but you also need to take things easy and at times take a back seat. If you take responsibility for yourself you will recognize what will help you at any given time. Act upon it, whether this is taking a rest or taking time out for yourself or spending time talking with others. Listen to what your body and mind tells you. Sometimes you might be thinking, 'I wish everybody would just go away', and at other times you really need to talk with someone you know and trust. These and other things are what you need at that time and if it is possible to do what will be helpful to you at that time, then do it. No one will take offence if you request some quiet time and it is most likely that your loved ones want to be with you when you need them.

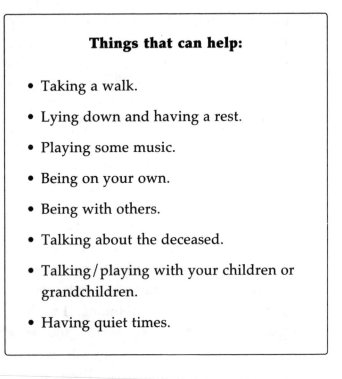

Things that can help:

- Taking a walk.

- Lying down and having a rest.

- Playing some music.

- Being on your own.

- Being with others.

- Talking about the deceased.

- Talking/playing with your children or grandchildren.

- Having quiet times.

Your faith and beliefs

A person's faith can be a huge comfort. Being part of a religious community can be reassuring and can help you feel that the death was part of God's plan. However, equally, a tragic death can cause you to question your faith. If you have a crisis of faith, don't worry about it; it is probably a temporary state, while you try to come to terms with your loss. It might be helpful to read a holy book to find some solace in words of wisdom. Religion recognizes the full circle of life and death and religious thought can sometimes help give meaning to our experiences. Handing over to a higher power can also be a relief for some people. Praying, meditating, singing a hymn or chanting might also help. Mourning rituals can be particular to a faith and can be a source of further solace.

I'm a Buddhist. Before my partner died I read to him from the Tibetan Book of the Living and Dying. We both believe that death is part of life and the idea that life is transient. I wanted to help him with his transition. My beliefs did help me enormously when he died, but of course I grieved like everyone else – I'm human.

Geoff

You don't need to follow a conventional religion to have faith in a greater dimension to life. Faith can be a very personal, or different, thing. You may hold spiritual or philosophical rather than religious beliefs. Some parts of religion might appeal to you and others not – like a belief in the afterlife, which is consoling for many people. Be comforted by what you find meaningful or uplifting.

You might not have a religious faith, but we all have things that we believe in and things we value. Perhaps you really value your family or other loved ones. You might love your work, your home or your ability or talents. Our beliefs can give meaning to our lives. Beliefs can be things like 'we reap what we sow in life' or that it's important to think positively, or that life is basically good. Reaffirm beliefs you have by asking yourself what beliefs you hold about life and death that could help you now. What do you value about your life that is still with you?

Values and beliefs might include:

- All things must pass away – life is transient.

- Death is part of life.

- I am a happy person and I manage to get over difficulties.

- Good times will come again.

- Nature is healing.

- I love, and I am loved.

- My religious/spiritual/philosophical beliefs sustain me.

- I believe in the afterlife.

- I believe in heaven.

- I believe that people I loved are still around me and help me at difficult times.

- I believe in God.

- I believe in angels.

- I believe that I have the strength to get through this and heal.

- My family and friends are very important to me.

- My work is important to me.

How many of the beliefs and values are true for you? Spend some time thinking about what you have in your life and let it reassure you. Now is the time to use your beliefs and value systems to buoy you up. Think of how you got through times of hardship or difficulty in the past and how you managed. What helped you at the time? If other people helped you what was it that they said or did?

Taking it slowly

In the early days of a significant bereavement it is important that you take things slowly. People can be incredibly kind and sensitive towards the bereaved and this is hugely reassuring, as are their words of comfort, and perhaps their support makes it possible for you to rest at times. It is important that you don't try to do too much – the likelihood is that you are unable to cope with many practical matters. They are likely to feel meaningless to you presently. It is not a good time to make any major decisions, so keep decision making to a minimum if possible or delegate minor decisions. Take things step by step. It might be enough at the moment to get through the day. And remind yourself that things will get better with time.

Be comforted, difficulties dealing with practical matters will pass, and piece by piece you will recover your life – but right now accept any useful offers from others. Partners might also be affected by the death and mutual love and care are required. You can help with each other's morale. If a child has died then both parents need support and comfort from family and friends. Parents, grandparents, other children and members of the family might also be grieving and it is important to recognize everyone's pain and to listen to what each person has to say.

It is hard to think of bereavement in positive terms but it can bring those who survive closer together and it is an opportunity to cherish each other. Long talks into the night could find you talking in great depth about things that you thought you had forgotten. Grief can break down barriers that the years have created and can be a bonding experience.

Many people say they found some consolation when they were able to choose something (however small) from the belongings of the person who died. Talking to the deceased or sending them loving thoughts can be a comfort. Some report – frequently quite adamantly – that the person is around them both in the early stages of grieving and at special times (like anniversaries) later on. For instance, they say that they can smell a certain smell they associate with the person or they can hear the person's voice. Whatever gives you comfort and reassurance must be good as long as it doesn't cause you or others any harm.

Although no losses are exactly the same, sometimes it can be helpful to talk with someone who has had a similar loss. Their understanding and advice could prove invaluable. It will reassure you that you can survive this – they did and you can too.

MYTH: It is a good thing to clear out the deceased person's belongings straight away.

FACT: No. It is better for everyone if you wait a little while. Trust your own instincts – you will know when it is the right time for you and others. Certainly wait until after the funeral.

Family, children, love and cuddles

Let others who love you comfort you. Accept love and understanding from family, friends and colleagues. It can be a comfort to talk and to be listened to but don't forget the healing powers of touch. Accept that cuddle from your partner or your child. If someone asks, 'What can I do to help?' Perhaps you could ask them to hold your hand or tell them 'I need a hug.'

We often try to hide our pain from children and try not to let them see us upset or crying but they aren't easily fooled. They will know if you are hurting and they will want to comfort you. It is okay to let your children see you upset. They are also likely to be upset; especially if it is someone they loved who has died and if they see you reining in your emotions then they are likely to feel that it is wrong for them to show theirs. If they see you cry then they will get the message that it is okay for them to cry, too. If your children ask you a direct question about the death answer them honestly, and, without elaborating, give them the information they ask for. It's infinitely better that they hear details from you or others close to them than from those who might not deal with things as sensitively. Families often try to protect each other from getting upset. They think that if one person gets upset then everyone will, but what is wrong with that? The family members or close friends who cry together and who aren't frightened of showing and sharing their emotions and vulnerabilities will feel closer than ever.

Cuddles and stroking each other's arms, or giving a massage are excellent ways of giving comfort. A head and shoulder massage will help you and others relax. Pets are a reassuring presence and give a sense of life's continuum. Stroking and playing with a pet is known to have therapeutic effects.

Q: Is it morbid to take children to the funeral of someone they loved?

A: No. Generally speaking, it is good to include children in the funeral proceedings when the person has been a significant loved one in their lives. It can help them with their grieving but use your own judgement on this.

Feed your soul

Try to take some form of exercise, such as a walk each day, if you can, ideally to a place with abundant greenery, like a park. Nature is soothing and research has shown that being around plant life helps lift depression. Making the effort is made easier if you have a dog that needs walking. Simple exercise releases chemicals called endorphins in our brains and bodies, and makes us feel happier and less stressed. If you don't want to go outside of the home for a few days then sitting in your garden will ensure you get fresh air in your lungs and will help with your breathing. Some people find that pottering in the garden offers some solace, but not everyone has a garden and if this is the case a walk in the park will have the same beneficial effects.

It can be helpful to listen to music. You might feel inclined to avoid any music that has associations with the person who died. However, if you are able to listen to music that evokes memories, it might help you to get in touch with your emotions and have a good cry. Reading poetry can be consoling. Susanne, a counsellor with many years of experience, suggests that mourners do simple tasks as a way of grounding themselves in the here and now. She said that one person she had seen who had recently been bereaved had found it therapeutic to make bread. 'There was something in the creating of the bread that she related was almost like giving birth – she could sense renewal in it, and it seemed to help her.'

Although it is a time when you need to rest more than usual, alternating between rest and productive tasks can help get a balance between your (at present) chaotic introspective inner world and your outer world. Manageable amounts of work can help ground you in the here and now.

I did more gardening following my father's death than I had ever done in my life. The garden looked beautiful. He had worked as a gardener for many years and he loved plants. I felt I was honouring him by tending the garden. He had often helped me with my garden. It helped me feel close to him and to feel that he was still around.

Jenny

Do whatever helps you cope

It will help you to cope with your feelings if you try to accept them rather than push them away or fight them. It is reasonable that you have a strong reaction to the death of someone you cared about. Try not to worry if at times you feel overwhelmed with grief. It will get easier but at the moment it is necessary for you to feel whatever you are feeling. It is your mind and body's way of coping as best they can. Feeling that you have the understanding of others is very helpful. You are likely to want to have your thoughts and feelings validated.

When you discover something that helps, then do it. For example, a woman who was a fan of yoga continued to do yoga every day when she was mourning the loss of her husband and she found that the child position was particularly comforting. (To do this, sit on your haunches, lean your torso forward, head to the floor, and arms back by your side. Breathe naturally and relax your body.) Bear in mind that it isn't disrespectful to enjoy something or have pleasure at a time of grieving, even when it involves laughter or feeling happy. It will help you with your grief. Life goes on and you need moments of respite.

Part 2:
Taking Control –
The Next Steps

In Part 2 we will be looking at a time when you are perhaps in a different stage of grieving. As we have mentioned before it is impossible to give exact times of stages as we all grieve slightly differently, and the extent of our mourning can depend on factors like the severity of the situation before or at the time of death. This stage, which we can perhaps think of as a middle stage (when the initial shock has worn off), can have its own problems and challenges and yet you are likely to recognize changes in your mourning. The purpose of this part of the book is to offer support and advice for the kind of things that might be happening to you now. We will be offering help firstly with how you might be affected on an emotional level and we will then move on to practical matters.

You have come through the first stages of grieving, when perhaps you weren't able to think straight and you felt stretched to your limits. Give yourself a huge pat on the back and be proud of yourself. The pain you felt just after your loved one's death might have been almost unbearable at the time but you have managed to survive this far. You might have been overwhelmed by grief and felt inconsolable and it could have seemed as if you would never be able to cope, but you did. It could be useful to remind yourself of this when you find things hard in the future because it could help you to move forward a little more. It might help to say to yourself, 'I got through that really horrendous time and, although I know I am still grieving, things will gradually get easier.'

5

Different types of death and the challenges they present

Suffering any loss is difficult, and while it perhaps isn't useful to think of any particular type of death as being more painful than another, there are types of loss that, by their nature, have their own particular difficulties. These kinds of bereavements include suicide, death through violence and the death of a child. If you have been affected by such a loss then you could benefit from seeking some expert help from agencies and therapists who specialize in this area. It is impossible to cover all the different types of painful losses, and the following are just a few, but perhaps they have some relevance to your own situation.

A dramatic death

A loss that takes place in a sudden or dramatic way can feel impossible to bear and sometimes the grief you feel can become more complicated than when people die in more natural circumstances. If we lose a person close to us from violence or suicide we might be more likely to feel terrible guilt or anger. If we lose a child we might think things like 'Why was our child taken from us – did we do something to deserve this?' The grief we feel might be too big for even the most loving of family and friends and it would be sensible to seek specialist help.

Coping with the death of a child

Having to cope with the death of a child is one of the hardest and saddest things that can happen to a person. It can be heartbreaking. It goes against all our natural instincts to protect and nurture our children. Children are vulnerable and depend on us to survive and when they don't make it we might feel that we have failed the child and perhaps that we have failed as a parent. Usually, nothing could be further from the truth. The love you feel for your child attests to that. You most likely did all you could and you mustn't blame yourself. Even when we are older and our child is an adult, we still see them as our child.

Often people talk about their child's short life as 'a life unlived' and that they were 'taken from us' and perhaps, more than any other type of death, the death of a child might feel like punishment. Perhaps you have had thoughts like 'He didn't really have a life' or 'I'll never see her grow up to become an adult.' We are acutely aware of all that we, and they, will miss and it can feel as if a part of ourselves dies with the child.

My son, Jack, died after being attacked by a young lad with a knife outside a nightclub. There was no apparent reason for the attack other than he was in the wrong place at the wrong time. Jack was 28. It felt at the time, and it still does, like a senseless waste of his life.

Gordon

More than any other kind of loss it might feel harder to 'let go' of a child. You might feel that you never want to let go and that is fine, too. You certainly need never forget them; they will always be in your heart and memory. Remember, **there are no wrongs in grieving**. We all deal with what happens as best we can. Life has presented you with a heartbreaking experience and if you feel angry then it is little wonder. In Part 5, Chapter 18 you will find helplines relating to child death. *The Child Death Helpline* offers a lifetime of emotional support for those whose lives have been touched by the death of a child. The organization writes: 'Callers often find it comforting to talk and describe the worries and emotions that unexpectedly overwhelm them or return after many years.'

The death of a baby

Sudden Infant Death Syndrome (SIDS), also called 'cot death', is most likely to affect babies from one to six months of age. It is a great source of worry for parents as it often strikes when a child appears to be in good health and when the parents have taken great care to provide a safe environment for their child.

The booklet, *When a Baby Dies* (suddenly and unexpectedly), from the UK's *Foundation for the Study of Infant Deaths* (FSID – details in Part 5, Chapter 18) explains what happens after the sudden death of a baby. It contains an informative frequently asked questions and answers section.

Parents might have to endure an inquest into the death and a postmortem examination of the baby to determine how they died, as well as an interview with the police. Of course, as necessary as these steps might be, they can be a further source of distress to parents and add to thoughts that they might have done something wrong. If this happens to you, try not to see it in this way and think of it as formalities that unfortunately need to be carried out.

The FSID website (**www.sids.org.uk**) affirms that 'Cot death can occur at any time of the year, in any place and in any family' and 'research has led to the view that cot death is seldom due to a single cause.'

Most useful of all to parents who have lost a child through a cot death, is the *Care of Next Infant* (CONI) programme, set up by FSID to support parents whose lives have been directly or indirectly affected by cot death tragedy. The programme takes place in hospitals and community health centres by midwives, paediatricians, GPs and health visitors. FSID also has a 'befriender' system whereby parents who have experienced cot death offer support to those whose lives have been affected by cot death more recently.

Stillbirths

Another traumatic way of losing a child is when a child is stillborn or dies soon after the birth. *The Stillbirth and Neonatal Death Society* (SANDS) in the UK offers support for bereaved parents and their families when their baby dies in these circumstances. It has a national helpline service; a national network of local self-help groups run by and for bereaved parents as well as informative publications.

Often the mother gives birth naturally to the stillborn baby and the stress and sadness the parents have to endure is beyond imagination. All the expectations the couple might have had from carrying the baby to full term have been cruelly thwarted and instead of taking the baby home in their arms, as most people do, the couple face saying goodbye to their precious child. The emotional adjustments required of them are immense. The couple had most likely been looking forward to the birth with great excitement and joy and the reality has been very different. It is considered to be very important for the parents' mental health and emotional recovery that they spend time with their baby, holding, dressing and naming him or her. Many choose to have a photograph of the baby to keep for the future. There is research to suggest that parents who choose not to spend time bonding with the child regret it later and have a much harder time grieving.

Sudden death

If we have warning that death is approaching, when someone has been diagnosed as terminally ill for example, it can, to some extent, prepare us. However, when a person dies suddenly, and unexpectedly, we have no time to prepare. We are denied the opportunity to tell the person that we love them or to say goodbye. It can be a horrific shock when death comes out of the blue and it shakes our world. Sudden death can happen through an (often senseless) act of violence, a fatal accident, or a previously undiagnosed illness. When death comes suddenly, our world changes overnight, and shock is inevitable.

It can be particularly distressing to know that a loved one died in violent circumstances. This might have been a murder, another violent situation or a fatal accident and can leave us in a state of tremendous shock. In such circumstances we might feel great anger and initially want revenge, or suffer anxiety or panic attacks. Alternatively, we might feel guilt, 'I should have been there to protect her' – even when this was impossible. Perhaps you lie awake at night thinking about how the person died, replaying details over and over in your mind. Or you might have nightmares. If this happens to you, know that these are temporary emotions and they will pass. However, if they go on for a considerable time, please get some help. When we try to deal with situations as big as this alone, it can have adverse effects on our relationships with others. If we are feeling desperately unhappy and tortured over a difficult death then we are also likely to be snappy and unreasonable with people around us. Relationships might suffer under the strain, so accept when you need help and talk to your doctor.

Q. I'd like to set up a charity in my deceased son's name. How do I go about this?

A. Call *The Charity Commission Contact Centre* on: 0845 300 0218, or look at the website: **www.charity-commission.gov.uk**, to learn how to register as a charity.

Suicide

The suicide of a loved one can be incredibly hard to cope with. Often, close friends and family are deeply affected by a suicide. Until fairly recently, attempted suicide was regarded as a crime, hence the term 'committed suicide'. How can we understand suicide? It goes against our human instinct – to survive at all costs. We'll 'fight to save our lives' and 'survive against all odds'. How then, can we make sense of an act of self-destruction? Often, much is left to guesswork. We are left with questions such as 'What was the person thinking when they chose to kill themselves?' and 'How had their life got so bad that they chose to end it?' More often than not suicide is not a rational, thought-out decision; it is more likely to be carried out when the person isn't thinking straight and is in a disturbed state of mind.

Needless to say, people left behind might feel terrible remorse and guilt. They might feel that they should have somehow been able to help the person and prevent their death. These kinds of feelings are made worse if there have been arguments and bad feeling between the person who killed themselves and the mourners.

I had cut off my friendship with Andy because he was a heroin addict. We'd been very close at one time but I hadn't seen him for a while. I had heard he had got clear of drugs but he visited me at home one day and he was behaving very strangely. I had to ask him to go because my young children were there at the time and I thought he must still be on drugs. Next thing I heard was that he had died from an overdose and I felt really guilty. I felt that I should have helped him more.

Gill

Often the person has suffered from depression and might have attempted to end their life, unsuccessfully. However, it is not only depressed people who kill themselves.

Some possible reasons for suicide include:

- Illness or disability – they might have felt a burden to others.

- Depression or mental illness (like schizophrenia – hearing voices instructing them to end their life).

- Something has convinced them that life is not worth continuing – they might have been in psychological pain following a trauma or a crisis.

- Low self-esteem – a sense of worthlessness.

- A build-up of anger, resentment and frustration.

- A momentary decision.

Sometimes it is hard to tell if it was actual suicide or an accident. If the person was taking either prescribed or other drugs, they might have taken too many pills or overdosed in another way. There are a lot of unknowns around suicide that make it very difficult and painful for the survivors. When someone dies of illness there is a cause and a reason for the death but when someone ends their own life many questions are left unanswered.

If a person close to you has taken his or her own life and you feel deeply troubled by it, it is often beneficial to talk with someone outside the family. It might be wise to enlist the help of a local counsellor. You could access a list of counsellors through the *British Association for Counselling and Psychotherapy* (BACP), or your doctor's surgery might provide counselling. Ask your doctor or contact an agency like *Survivors of Bereavement by Suicide* (SOBS), on their UK national helpline number: 0870 2413337 (seven days a week 9 a.m. to 9 p.m.). They also provide support groups with people who have been similarly bereaved, in various locations (currently 30 locations), residential events, support days and a quarterly newsletter. You might like to look on the SOBS website (*see* Part 5, Chapter 18 for further details).

An anticipated death

Sometimes the death of our loved one is anticipated, as with terminal illness. When the person is ill for some time, we watch their health deteriorate. We perhaps see our loved one's prolonged suffering and get worn down by it. Later, we might feel haunted by how the person suffered 'a painful, lingering death'. The emotional turmoil this can cause might at times feel almost unbearable. It can feel unfair and cruel and you feel that the person didn't deserve it. A long illness can bring up all sorts of feelings and yet we are likely to feel that we should, to some extent, put on a brave face for the dying person's sake. In these circumstances the close family and friends of the dying person might feel that they have already started the grieving process, but in other ways they are also likely to hold hope that the person will survive and find it hard to accept that death is near. On one level they might want them to go to save them further pain and anguish, but on another they don't want to lose the person.

When a death is anticipated it does give us the opportunity to talk with the person about what arrangements they would like for their funeral and other matters, and to say goodbye.

If this happens it can be a comfort later. (Although it has to be said that not everyone is comfortable or wants to talk about these matters even with those they love.) However, when the person dies, life can feel suddenly empty because we no longer have the busy distractions of visiting (perhaps in hospital or a nursing home) and caring for the person in the way we did when they were still alive. We might initially feel huge relief or euphoria when they die because they are freed of suffering but sometimes we also feel guilt that we feel this way. To help you understand your feelings try saying to yourself something like 'I loved … very much and although I am very sad about their passing, I'm glad that they are now out of the pain and suffering – they are now at peace.'

The death of a parent

Although it is usually something that we have the longest time to prepare for, no matter what age we are, when a parent dies it is highly likely to have a profound effect on us and it is not only those who had a close and loving relationship with their parents who feel the weight of loss.

People say things like 'I don't understand it – I was never particularly close to my mother/father and yet I felt devastated when they died.' The reason we usually have strong feelings after a parent dies is that they have been a huge presence in our lives. For a start, usually, they have known us all our lives. We relied heavily, often almost solely, on them for our survival in the early years and our identities are tied up with theirs. We share the same genes. They perhaps knew us better and longer than anyone else.

Of course, how we react will have something to do with the kind of relationship we had with them. Often we revert back to having childlike feelings towards our parent after they die. If the parent was domineering or critical then we might have mixed feelings; we are perhaps more likely to feel anger as well as sadness. There might be relief that we can now lead a life of our own without their opinions or criticism. On the other hand, if we were very close to our parent and always knew we had their support and unconditional love, we are likely to feel more like we have been abandoned. As children, when we were dependent on parents, we feared they might not be there when we needed them (perhaps in the middle of the night when we were scared) and when they die, through no fault of their own, they do leave us and we might once more respond in a childlike way.

How deeply we are affected by a significant loss, like the death of a parent, might depend on what else is happening to us in our lives at the time. If we are in a happy relationship or have a family of our own with lots of love and support, then of course this helps. If, however, we are in the middle of a divorce, are feeling alone and without support, then it is going to be harder. However, do remember that there is always help available. There really is no need to suffer your heartache alone. More often than not there are people in similar situations, having problems with coming to terms with difficult bereavements. Perhaps there are local support groups where you can share experiences and know that you have the understanding of people with similar grief problems. With the right support you will be able to get on with your life.

6

Later symptoms
of grief

You can expect to be feeling many of the symptoms of grief that we previously looked at, such as sadness and anxiety, but perhaps not so intensely or as often. It is natural that you will feel great sadness at times when you think of the deceased. There is nothing wrong with that. It is natural, understandable and healthy. It takes time to gain an emotional stability but it comes. Think again about all the feelings you had at the time immediately following your loved one's death and you will see that already you feel differently.

Anxious and helpless feelings might also have lessened but it has to be remembered that you might have to learn new skills and also need to do more, if you no longer have a partner to share things with. Perhaps at times you feel overwhelmed with all the things that need attention. If you are adjusting to life without the person around on a daily basis, remind yourself of this. Anger, guilt and depression can all come to the surface when you find it a real struggle coping on your own if, for instance, you are a mother with young children to bring up alone, or you are an older person who doesn't find it easy to do things on your own. Try to remind yourself of what you are managing rather than focusing on what you are finding hard, and give yourself credit.

Let's remind ourselves of what was happening in the first stages of your grief and what you survived. You were likely to be in shock – nature's way of helping you cope with the enormity of what had happened. At first it might have been very hard for you to accept the death – hard to believe that the person you cared deeply about had gone. Our immediate reaction is often one of disbelief 'They can't be dead – it hasn't happened.' Everything might have felt unreal, perhaps different from anything else you had experienced before, so you might have appeared to be carrying on as normal, keeping busy. Perhaps you felt great sadness at the funeral and it was cathartic to some extent or you might have still been too numb to feel sadness and felt an icy calm. The main indications of stage one were likely to be:

- Shock.

- Denial.

- Feeling everything is unreal/the world is standing still.

- Signs of shock and stress in our minds (can't sleep, disorientated thoughts, lack of concentration).

- Signs of shock and stress in our bodies (achy body, restlessness, listlessness).

Remember, although we can set out different stages in mourning, they don't happen in a straightforward way. In the second – or middle – stage of mourning, you are likely to have *some*, but not all, of the symptoms of the first stage and even when you are in later stages of grieving you might, at times, go back to feelings that you had in the first stages, after the death of your loved one. However, generally speaking feelings are usually more manageable than they were first time around. They can be less intense and therefore a little easier to cope with. It is inevitable that there will be overlap; you will have good days, when you recognize that you are feeling better, and bad days when you might wonder if your life will ever get back on an even par.

In Part 3, we will look at how it is possible to move on with your life and invest in new relationships and find new meaning in your world, but before you get to this point, you need to come to terms with your changed circumstances.

> *We have a family farm and my son was the manager until he got cancer. His death was a terrible blow to the family. Sometimes when something is difficult to sort out, I've felt grief, anger and frustration all at once and have hardly been able to contain the emotions I'm feeling. I feel like screaming out and, on a few occasions when I've been alone, I have done. It helps.*

Jake

Where you might be now

Perhaps in the months after the funeral things seem a little more stable and you feel more in control of your life, but not always. For some people, grief can get worse in the period following the funeral. If this happens to you, you might imagine that the pain is going to get worse forever but this isn't so, it will get better.

Maybe you have noticed a shift from how you felt when you were in the early crisis stage. You might have already had to deal with some practical matters such as helping to arrange the funeral and consulting a solicitor. You have come through the first days, weeks and months after the death of the one you mourn. It has been far from easy but you have perhaps discovered strengths you never knew you had.

Realistically, there are likely to be more difficulties to come but, hopefully, with the help of other people and by getting back to some daily routines, you can see a light at the end of the tunnel and feel some hope for the future. You got through a very traumatic time. Keep on reminding yourself that you feel better now than you did and that things will continue to improve. You might still be struggling at times but you can see some changes. You have got very acute time of crisis. You have made it to this point. Keep reminding yourself that generally you feel a bit better than you did and that things will continue to improve.

What to expect right now

What can you realistically expect at the moment, say two, three or more months down the line? It is always good to look at what you expect of yourself and other people to test if this is realistic. While it is perhaps good to give yourself some challenges, like getting out and meeting friends or returning to work, it is also important that what you expect is realistic. Perhaps at times you expect too much of yourself. You need to pay attention to how you are feeling. Are you feeling well or strong enough to attend a function? Are you eating and sleeping better? You can monitor how you are better than anyone, and you will recognize progress and signs of recovery as well as when you might be pushing yourself too much. Remind yourself when things get hard that you are still grieving and be patient. The support and comfort of family and friends might continue to be very important to you. Try not to be afraid of asking for ongoing help and support.

Perhaps you are expected to return to work and carry on as before the bereavement, but you might not feel ready. Be honest and discuss this with your employers. You could perhaps negotiate a gradual return to work, where you work fewer hours for a while. Some people find that returning to work is beneficial because it gives their life structure. You are taking tentative steps some days and larger ones the next. You will help yourself if you build some coping strategies (get to know what helps you) and take things at your own pace, doing ordinary daily tasks like cooking a meal or walking the dog.

For some people this is an easier time, but not for everyone. If you were unable to feel the reality of the death early on you might start to feel it at a later date, when other people seem to have moved on, and that can present problems. You might think that other people have got over the death and ask yourself 'Why haven't I?' Possibly people have stopped calling you to check that you are all right or to ask if they can do anything to help. You might feel more able to deal with some practical matters, such as sorting out the deceased person's belongings. Equally, you might not (there are no hard and fast rules) but, at times, you probably still appreciate support and advice.

So, what can you do if people appear to have withdrawn their support? Sometimes all you need to do is just tell people how you are feeling and that you would appreciate some help. We are all guilty at times of thinking that other people are clairvoyants and that they know exactly how we feel and what we need. Unfortunately this isn't true and sometimes we need to spell it out. It isn't 'weak' to let people know about our vulnerabilities. In fact it takes a lot of strength to say, 'I'm still struggling here, and I would appreciate your understanding.' Don't forget to show your appreciation and give people thanks and praise where it is due. Remember, they are helping because they care about you and want the best for you but they are probably hoping for signs that you are managing some things on your own, so show them that you are trying at times to manage and that at other times you really appreciate a helping hand.

Emotional pain and support

You are still going to feel emotionally sensitive – feelings for your loved one don't just go away after the funeral takes place. But, hopefully these feelings are, for the majority of the time, less debilitating. Because you are likely to spend more time alone or with less people months after the death, painful feelings of anger and guilt might creep in. At this time, you are probably trying to make sense of the loss by asking yourself questions about whether you or another person were somehow to blame.

Perhaps you are wrangling with your own conscience or with the unfairness of life or perhaps you are just missing the person who died. People often talk about yearning or pining for the person, longing to see, hear and hold them. Sometimes people find it a comfort to keep an article of clothing that holds a smell of the deceased. There is nothing wrong or macabre about this. It is like having a transition object, similar to the comfort of a much-loved teddy or blanket, as a child. It perhaps enables us to feel that the person is still near to us. Usually, a time comes when we no longer need the reminder and we are able to part with it, but not always.

Remember, there are no rules in mourning; it is more a case of whatever helps us get by and ultimately to recover.

So, you can expect to still feel pain at times but, bit by bit, you will sense signs of recovery. A sign that things are changing is when you find yourself appreciating what is around you, something you have been unaware of in your grief. This might be noticing something of beauty in the world, like a sunset or budding plants in springtime, or a piece of music that moves you, or finding yourself laughing again for the first time in a while.

If you do have the continued support of friends and family, they might suggest that it is time you started to go out and socialize and perhaps join them for a meal. While it is sound advice you might not feel ready and feel inclined to refuse but try to socialize a little if you can – if you have lost a partner, home can feel a lonely place. If you are single, sometimes it helps to move in with a friend or family member for a while if this is practical. Trust your instincts on what is appropriate and helpful to you and other people who are grieving.

Remember that advice is not always good advice. People might readily give their advice (or opinions) about what they would do in certain situations or when you 'should' be returning to work or moving home. With the very best of intentions the advice they offer might not be the best for you. To help you distinguish between useful advice and not so useful advice try asking yourself, 'Who do I trust and think of as sensible and wise?' 'Whose advice have I tried and tested in the past?' 'Who knows me well and has my interests at heart?' 'Am I in the frame of mind at the moment that I can trust my own judgement or instincts?' (Remember, you are the one in charge.)

Children and grief

Naturally, children who have lost a parent, grandparent or other close family member or friend might be quite clingy for a while. They might worry that you are going to die and leave them too. Children have vivid imaginations and they might even worry that they caused the person's death because they were 'bad' in some way. Do encourage children to talk about their feelings and share yours with them. Let them see you cry and show them you are upset at times, to encourage them to express their own emotions freely. They are likely to need a lot of reassurance and attention for a while and plenty of patient attention. You might like to contact *Winston's Wish* or *Edward's Trust* to get support for your child or children (see Part 5 for details).

You will still be having frequent thoughts about the deceased. The pain of the loss is perhaps less acute, but it is still painful. You will still feel sad and at times feel it is difficult to cope, but take comfort in knowing you have come far to reach where you are now.

MYTH: Children never get over a major bereavement in the family, like the death of a parent.

FACT: It's often said that children are resilient and it's true. Of course, the death of a parent, sibling or grandparent can be devastating at the time but with the love and support of other members of the family and perhaps outside support, too, they will, in time, get over it. It is important that children are helped to keep the person's memory alive.

Changes in mourning

We are all different and so we have different responses to the death of someone we cared about. Months after the death you might recognize a shift in your grieving. It might just be that you are managing to do more. For some people the changes are obvious but for others they're more subtle – it can be details such as your sleeping has improved or that you no longer have a numb distracted feeling. Of course, if you feel less numb you might be more in touch with your feelings and perhaps the full pain of the loss will affect you now – just when you hoped that things would get easier. Remember to tell yourself daily: **There are no hard and fast rules in grieving, and feelings I have today will pass – things will get easier.**

You are having to accept the sad reality that the person has gone and that they are not coming back. This is too much to take in at first, when we really can't believe it is true, but in this middle stage you are trying to come to terms with that loss and also have to make a life for yourself without the person. This can require adjustments, on both an emotional and practical level, and it is a gradual process that takes time. Perhaps you feel achingly lonely at times or feel the weight of responsibility. You might have had to take on roles that you didn't have when the person was alive, for example, financial responsibility for paying the bills or practical things like household maintenance. If you have lost a spouse and have children, you might miss consulting your spouse about the children's upbringing and everyday family affairs. We miss people who have died in many ways.

Not everyone's pattern of grieving fits into the kind of pattern set out by experts. While we might feel emotions like anger and guilt in the early stages of bereavement, they are most likely to come back to us in the months after the death when we are perhaps more alone with our thoughts. Strong feelings can come at any time. You might find yourself struggling with a difficult job in the house (something your partner might have done when they were alive) and find yourself breaking down in frustration and anger or suddenly picturing the person you loved on their deathbed and feel overwhelmed with sadness and wish you had spent more time with them when they were alive.

It is common and natural to feel emotions such as guilt, remorse and anger while we work things through. Many of the feelings you initially felt (but not all) are likely to still affect you, at least at times. They are likely to come and go as you adjust to your changed circumstances.

You might still have:

- Feelings of helplessness (at times).

- Physical problems (for instance, disturbed sleep and lack of appetite).

- Negative, self-defeating thoughts ('I can't do this – how am I supposed to carry on?').

You might also have new feelings such as:

- Loneliness.

- Tiredness.

- Feeling burdened by responsibilities.

- Depression.

- Difficulty adjusting to life without the person.

In the months after the funeral you could be trying to adjust to a life that involves huge changes. Be patient with yourself. Take things day by day and when you do manage a new challenge, however small, say 'Well done' to yourself and see it as a huge achievement and proof that you are coping and moving forward. Some people find it consoling to think of the deceased being with them and wishing them well. Sometimes people talk to the person who has died and find it therapeutic. Remember, it is important that you do things in your own way and anything that helps – as long as it is not harming anyone else – is fine. You can send your love to the deceased at any time. It might make you feel better and a little closer to them.

I often talk to my friend Lucy, who died in a car accident, and because she was part of a group of close friends from secondary school, who did a lot of things together, we'll often talk about her, the kind of things she did, and wonder what she would do or say in a certain situation.

Gemma

How we cope with change generally

How we cope with our mourning sometimes relates to how we cope with change generally. Are you someone who adapts to change easily? If you find change hard then you might have a more troubled time. You can test this by thinking about times in your life when you had to deal with change. Did you see the change as a challenge? How did you cope? What does it say about you that you were able to adjust to the changes?

If you are not good with change then you might find the changes that bereavement brings more difficult. It might sound rather negative to focus on difficulties you have with change at this time but actually it can be very helpful to understand how we react to different situations because we can then work with this. It can help us accept what we are experiencing. We can think 'No wonder I am responding in this way – I find change difficult and now my life has changed dramatically and quite suddenly, I realize that it will take time for me to adjust.'

A shift is made when we move from being the victims of change (in as much as we have no control over the events) to making temporary or permanent changes of our choosing that are more helpful to us. This might involve arrangements for the children such as changing their schools nearer to home, or organizing a home help, or getting help with the management of debts (contact details for the Consumer Credit Counselling Service can be found in Part 5, Chapter 18). When we are able to make changes for the better it empowers us.

There is no doubt that bereavement challenges us in many ways: emotionally, physically, and in our resourcefulness. Here are some possible responses to challenges:

- When you find yourself thinking, 'I can't do this' – give it a try.

- Ask for help at the time.

- Learn how to do it (this might be something like computer skills or how to load a dishwasher).

- Do things in your own time – don't put yourself under any more pressure.

- Don't put yourself down and say things to yourself like 'I'm useless'.

- Be kind and patient with yourself.

- Congratulate yourself when you see a challenge through, however small.

7

What you and those around you might be feeling

The period before the funeral and the period after the funeral are often quite different. As we have seen, in the period before, we hardly have time to grieve. There is a flurry of activity, we might feel numb and go into shock. We are often surrounded by people and inundated with offers of help. Perhaps in the months after the funeral, people begin to get on with their own lives and offers of help are less forthcoming. It is also after the funeral, during the first week or so, when we begin to truly grieve and we go from that point to the end of grieving (some people say, that for them, grieving never truly stops, but certainly you can expect the pain to be less intense and more manageable as time goes by).

After the funeral

Coming to terms with a death can be a slow process and we mustn't be hard on ourselves if at times we appear to take two steps forward and then two steps back. The only way that you can know how others are feeling is by asking them and talking freely to each other. You and the other mourners are likely to be feeling that sometimes you are okay and doing well, and at other times it might feel like things are falling apart again. You need to try to be patient with yourself and each other and give the message that it is all right to share how you are feeling. It is easy to struggle on without confiding in each other so try to keep in touch and talk about how things are for all of you.

> **MYTH:** *The funeral took place a few months ago and my life should have gone back to normal by now.*
>
> **FACT:** Beware of 'shoulds' and 'musts' (whether self-imposed or from others). Remember you are dealing with things as best you can at any given moment.

Different ways of mourning

We all mourn differently. We might be able to offer mutual support, which would be marvellous, but we often don't live up to our expectations or fulfil our ongoing needs.

People from the same family can have very different ways of grieving. One person might be struggling with their emotions but it won't be obvious to other people; they have perhaps decided, 'I am just going to get on with it', while another person is more debilitated by their grief and is obviously struggling. Communication between the two can become tricky. You might think that you *should* have come to terms with the death while they might be burying unresolved feelings and be in denial. Perhaps you are getting the message from some people that you have grieved enough and should be moving on.

However, denying our pain can lead to complicated mourning. We may need to accept that while some people appear to grieve for a short time only, it takes other people longer to get over a bereavement. While some mourn the passing of a loved one for a few months before they are able to return to some kind of normality in their lives, other people grieve for a year to two years or longer, and it helps when we try to understand that it's okay for us all to grieve in our own way and in our own time.

There are many contributing factors to the length of time people grieve and the intensity of their grieving. These include:

- How adaptable you are to change.

- How close you were to the person who died.

- How dependent you were on the person.

- If there was 'unfinished business' with the person.

- How you perceive the person's life (for example, was it a 'good' life?).

- Your thoughts about your relationship with the person.

- The circumstances of the death.

Ongoing support

In the first few months of bereavement friends and family are usually very supportive. As time goes by, you could find the emotional or practical support of others less forthcoming or not enough. The reality is that offers of help, such as running errands or picking up children from school, might become less frequent. People probably still care very much but they are likely to be drawn back to the demands of their own lives. Another possibility is that some people's expectations of mourning don't fit with your grieving pattern – they might think that you should be managing by now, and this can be hurtful. You might understand that friends and other members of the family need to put their energies elsewhere but it can still be very upsetting. You might feel abandoned and that they don't care. If you feel that no one understands anymore, it can make you desperately unhappy. Try not to take it as a sign that there is something wrong with you; try instead to think that those people helped for a time – as long as they were able – and thank them for the help they gave, and seek help elsewhere.

It could be that you are feeling that you don't want to be a burden to other people, and you might say things to your family like 'No, I won't come to you at Christmas because I'll only get upset, and upset everybody else', imagining that it will be worse for them if you break down than if you stay away, which isn't necessarily so. Try talking to them about possible scenarios. Instead of deciding you won't go to a family gathering or holiday tell them there is a possibility that you might become upset and ask them how they would feel about that. Keep communication flowing.

If you start to feel that friends and family are no longer able to offer you the emotional support you need, then it could be beneficial to see a counsellor privately. (Look in Yellow Pages under 'counselling' or, alternatively, register with a bereavement care counselling service such as *Cruse*). It might be time to look for practical support elsewhere, too. You might consider (if finances allow) hiring a cleaner, sending your washing to a laundry service or finding a babysitter or nursery care. These are steps to gradual independence.

Take reassurance from what you have managed to date. It shows you what you can manage in the future. You have tapped into inner resources and you can continue to accept any help that is offered to you that you need.

Faith in life

If you are part of a religious community it could continue to be a comfort and means of support to you and your family. Whereas immediately following the bereavement, life perhaps felt unstable and even unsafe, your faith in life might slowly and surely begin to be restored. Perhaps you feel that there is light at the end of the tunnel. You are less shaken and are probably managing to do more. Possibly you have got into routines that you have found helpful. You have probably achieved more than you give yourself credit for. Maybe the relationships you have with other people have sustained you and you cherish those people you still have with you.

When someone dear to us dies, it takes both courage and faith to carry on. Sometimes we want to die too, the direction and purpose of our lives can seem unclear, and the pain is too hard to bear. Perhaps we feel that the person's death has left a huge gap in our lives and life holds little meaning for a while but, given time, our faith in life is restored and we realize that our life is not over. Usually, without forgetting the person who died, we find other people in the world to give our energies and love to. Having children to bring up can make us determined to make the best of things for their sake.

My grandchildren helped me to recover from the death of my son, the children's father. Watching them grow gives me a sense of the continuity of life. I learnt so much from them, not least how they live in the moment.

Jean

Beginning to enjoy life again

We all die – that is one of life's certainties – and we owe it to ourselves to make life as meaningful and enjoyable as we can. We cherished the person when they were alive and we can cherish memories of them now that they have died. It is often said of the deceased that they would want us to be happy. Of course they would like us to be happy. Even if the relationship we shared was a troubled one it is most likely that in death all pettiness dissolves. But to love is to suffer grief, when we lose the person. The poet Kahlil Gibran reminded us of this when he wrote in *The Prophet*:

> When you are sorrowful look again into your heart, and you will see that in truth you are weeping for that which has been your delight.

At some point we will rejoin life and, although we will never forget the person, we will focus our love and energies on the living. It is a gradual progression – you don't just wake up one day and find everything is wonderful again. It comes from slowly doing something both new and familiar, like going to see a film, or having a swim, and from appreciating and building on other relationships. Gradually we make a life that is worth living again.

Think of things you used to love doing – like dancing or watching comedy films – and let yourself enjoy it. Make a list of favourite things and start to re-introduce them one at a time. They don't have to be sophisticated; often it is the simple things in life that help us the most.

Tick the following list of things you might enjoy the most:

❏ Going out for a meal.

❏ Dancing.

❏ Yoga/meditation (both are relaxing and can be practised at home).

❏ Listening to music/buying CDs.

❏ Buying clothes.

❏ Joining a class in a subject that interests you (this is also a great way to meet new people).

❏ Gardening.

❏ Going for a walk (in the park, hills or mountains).

❏ Meeting friends for a coffee/drink.

❏ Chatting to friends on the phone.

❏ Swimming, golf or another sport.

The list is endless and perhaps you would like to make your own.

Dealing with difficult or disturbing recurring thoughts and emotions

As we have said before, grieving is not linear. If we tried to draw a pattern of grieving on a line chart, it might show a line dipping low and then rising a little higher and higher still and then dipping sharply again and so on. Sometimes something you see or something someone says can upset you again. It could be a chance meeting in the street when a friend from the past asks you how your partner or child is doing, not realizing that they have died, or a new teacher at your children's school innocently assuming that the children's daddy is alive. It can be something that stirs a memory: a place or a favourite song. It might be very painful and make you feel that you will never get over their death but you will. When something stirs you try to remember that at times you do feel okay and that it is normal to have difficult times and that strong evoked emotions will pass. Perhaps it will be helpful for you to remember the word 'accept' in relation to any feelings you have. **Say to yourself 'I accept all the feelings I have.'**

How your thoughts might affect you

Take note of your thoughts. It is now widely acknowledged that how we think affects our emotions, moods and behaviour. So if you constantly have negative, self-defeating thoughts, then you are more likely to feel bad and be unable to make things better for yourself. It is not *wrong* to have negative thoughts but they can be debilitating. Watch what you are thinking and ask yourself: 'Are my thoughts helping me?' 'Am I telling myself that I won't be able to cope?' 'Am I endlessly blaming myself?' 'Am I blaming others?' 'Am I saying that I can't possibly be happy now?' (Remember, if you are having suicidal thoughts and you haven't seen a doctor then it makes sense to do so).

Of course, having some negative thoughts after bereavement is normal but if you are constantly having negative, self-destructive thoughts, it means that something is wrong and that you might be turning the loss back on yourself in some way. You might be saying things like 'I should have been with them when they died' or 'I can't do this now I'm alone in the world.' Even little shifts in our thinking can make a big difference.

1. **Instead of:** 'I let my mother down – I wasn't with her when she died.'

   Try: 'I did what I could at the time – I'm not perfect, I had other commitments and she knew that I cared about her.'

2. **Instead of:** 'My life is over, now he has died – I'll never be happy again.'

   Try: 'I loved him very much and I can never replace him or what we had together. It will take time to come to terms with losing him but in time I will be able to move on and can be happy again.'

3. **Instead of:** 'I'm useless. Dan would have been able to do this – I should be able to.'

   Try: 'I'm not able to do this particular thing at the moment but I can learn to do it if necessary. If it is beyond me then I can either pay someone to do it or ask a friend or family member to help me. I am not useless – I manage to do other things. I am doing well.'

Realistic thoughts help us; negative thoughts are punitive and destructive. You can tell when you are being hard on yourself when you find your thoughts are full of 'shoulds' and 'musts'.

Affirmations

It sometimes helps to write a few affirmations down on business-size cards. You can place these around the house and carry them in your wallet to refer to at any time. They might say things that remind you of your strengths, along the lines of: 'I'm an able and resilient person', 'I move forward in my life without fear.' Or say something that reminds you of what is still good in your life: 'I'm surrounded by a family who love and support me.' Write down some affirmations that are meaningful to you and look at them when you are feeling low or need some encouragement.

MYTH: Affirmations don't work.

FACT: It is now widely acknowledged that our thoughts and beliefs – about ourselves, others and the world – are largely responsible for the reality we create. For example, if we think the world is a bad place, that is how we will experience it – we will put a bad slant on what happens to us. However, if we think of the world as a basically good place, then we are more likely to interpret things that happen to us in a way that helps us. Affirmations are about reminding ourselves about positive things – about ourselves, and about life in general.

What you can do to keep the person's memory alive

People sometimes worry that they will lose a sense of the person who died. They worry about not being able to remember accurately what they looked like, their smile, the sound of their voice, and other details that made them unique. Perhaps you have young children who have lost their parent and you want to give them ways of remembering them in the future. One way to do this is to make a memory book or box. A book can contain photos, newspaper cuttings, travel/theatre tickets, postcards and anything else that has relevance to your shared memories. Alternatively, you might prefer to make up a box to contain mementos of the person and your life together. If a child is finding it hard to talk about the death or the person who died it sometimes helps to give them a special box, and suggest they write their thoughts down and place them in the box. They can then decide if they would like to share these with you or another person or keep them as their own private thoughts. If they do choose to share, it can give you or others an insight into their thoughts and feelings.

When it comes to clearing the person's

belongings you might like to look for things that you or other people would like to keep. The person who died might have liked to draw or paint or write poems and left things that give pleasure to others and were unique to them. Another way is to give family members or close friends something that belonged to the deceased – something that says something about their life together. This could be something like a fishing rod or something else relating to a shared appreciation of a sport, or it might be a ring or another piece of jewellery that can be passed down through the generations or a piece of furniture or ornament. It doesn't have to be valuable in a monetary sense, it is more important that it has meaning for the receiver.

Why am I still crying?

Please don't ever feel bad about crying. Think of it as a sign of your love for the deceased and also as your body's way of letting go of distress and sadness. If you feel low or upset it will help to have a cry. Sometimes we tell ourselves 'I shouldn't still be crying at this stage – I should have moved on.' But you know what you need to do and what helps you. If you feel like crying, then you need to cry. When sadness is suppressed it can come out in other ways, such as emotional outbursts, illness or bitterness and that won't be good for anyone.

It is also important to continue to talk about your loved one with other people who will understand. Remember, there is a tendency for people to protect each other and if they think that they will upset you by talking about the deceased then they won't mention them, so let them know that it is still okay with you and that you enjoy talking and need to talk about the deceased.

MYTH: Crying is a sign of weakness.

FACT: Crying is a way in which humans express emotion. It is natural for us to cry when we are under stress or feeling sad and it helps us. People who regard crying as a sign of weakness are usually afraid of emotions – either their own, other people's or both.

Practical lifelines

Organizing your life and taking control

You might not have even noticed that you have been organizing your life and taking control. You have simply had to. Perhaps you have had to make sure that the children get to school, or that your partner and yourself have a cooked meal each day. Possibly you helped with practical arrangements for the funeral. If a partner has died then you probably have had to take over payment of bills, sole responsibility for children and maintenance of the house. It is probably hard for you to see how far you have come from the first days of losing your loved one, but the chances are, you have.

If you are older, then ideas about taking control might have little meaning. You might feel unable to do this for physical or other reasons. In this case taking control might mean making sure that you are receiving all the help you can get. Ask someone to contact Social Services on your behalf, to organize help such as meals on wheels, visits to day centres, a home help or health checks.

How are you physically?

After a few months, you can expect to suffer less of the physical signs of grief. Look at the list of symptoms on pages 8–9 in Part 1 and see how many apply to you now. The feeling of numbness you had initially, when you couldn't feel anything, is likely to have gone. The shock of the death may have gone, to some extent. The funeral will have taken place and the constant talking and thinking about the deceased in the period following the death might have eased a bit now. Because you are likely to feel less stressed, your body should feel less tired. However, for some people this is the time that the sadness of the loss fully hits them. Perhaps you have a cry when you think of the deceased. This is perfectly normal and it really is fine to have a cry at any stage of grieving, whether this is a month after the death or a year or more.

Returning to normal life

The demands of everyday life inevitably call you back after a while. You might be returning to work after some time off or getting out more. You might wonder how you are going to cope if people mention the death or whether you will burst into tears if someone offers their condolences. You can only test the waters a little and see how you manage. It might help you to picture in your mind the kind of things people might say to you and what you might say in reply. Practise responses and try to picture yourself coping. It might help you to write down and rehearse a 'script' of what you would like to say to people when they ask you certain questions or offer their condolences. This can be very helpful because it takes a little of the emotion out of the situation.

I live in a small village and, before my son died, I used to go into the nearest town to shop once a week but after he died I couldn't face going in because I kept bumping into people I knew and they would say how sorry they were to hear about his death and I'd get really upset. That was a year ago and things have got better now but I still avoid town when I feel low.

Sheila

Sheila had her own way of coping and no doubt you have found yours. You are doing really well – remind yourself of this. You are likely to have had to make huge adjustments to the changed circumstances of your life. Perhaps you are gradually reshaping your life. You might have become a widow or a widower and the death of your partner may mean that you now struggle financially or in other ways. Sex and intimacy might presently be absent in your life and looking for another partner is the furthest thing from your mind. You might miss the affection you shared with your partner. They would probably be the person you would turn to for comfort in other circumstances. Don't underestimate what you have been going through, and are still going through, but neither should you underestimate your achievements to date.

Looking after yourself

Try to continue to look after yourself. If you are now in a position where you are looking after other people, such as a parent or children, then it is easy to neglect your own needs. Try to get breaks where you can and remember to do things that you enjoy and that relax you. Indulge yourself with long soaks in the bath and if you can fit in a massage every now and then it will help to unknot any tension in your body. Also eat well and make sure you get enough sleep. If your sleep is still disturbed, continue to nap in the day if you can. You could discuss sleeping tablets with your GP, as short-term use of these can break bad sleep patterns and help you to return to more restful sleep.

For some people it helps to let things be less than perfect for a while. Maybe you are not up to making cooked meals, and convenience food will do or maybe you can be less fussy about tidiness in the house. For a time you might need to put your energies into just managing the basics. Give yourself breaks and don't be too demanding of yourself. For some people routine is very important but you will need to be the judge of what is important for you. Being active can take your mind off things, but it's important to get the balance right. Try to take note of what helps you. Some days you might feel like following a familiar routine but not on others.

After my mother died, I was very low for quite a while. At first I let things go around the house. Nothing seemed that important. But then I realized that when I did manage to get things done it seemed to help. Routine things like taking the children to school, doing the washing and cleaning gave an ordinariness to the day.

Emma

9

Practical and financial considerations

Assuming that by now the will has, or is, being dealt with and insurance monies have been claimed and a solicitor is dealing with other financial matters, what other practicalities follow months after the death?

Practical matters that might need attention

Some matters that might need attention include:

- Choosing a burial headstone or crematorium plaque.

- Sorting out and disposing of the person's belongings.

- Putting a property up for sale.

- Changing child arrangements.

- Arranging for the care of a surviving parent.

- Becoming the sole owner of a property or business.

Q. How do I go about investing money I've been left in a will?

A. It would be wise to look for an independent financial adviser – one who is authorized and regulated by the *Financial Services Authority*. For information about choosing an adviser look at the website: **www.consumerdirect.gov.uk**. You'll find local independent financial advisers in the Yellow Pages.

Financial matters

When you aren't sure how to go about something then get the advice of an expert. If you have inherited money and aren't sure how best to invest it, you might like to employ the services of an independent financial adviser (remember that financial advisers, who are employed by a company, are more likely to peddle their company's products and they might not be the best for you).

If you are selling a house then shop around estate agents and check what percentage of the sale they charge. Usually they can be knocked down, especially if they think they will lose your custom to a competitor if they aren't flexible. Shop around to find out who offers the best all-round service. Ask questions such as:

- How do they advertise their properties (local, national papers, internet etc.)?

- How many potential buyers does the service reach?

- Will they use photographs of the property to advertise it?

- Do they have specialist property lawyers as part of their service?

You could also look at ways to sell property on the internet.

Financial problems

If you have financial problems at this difficult time it is an added blow. Perhaps you have lost the person who was the main wage earner in the home. What do you do in a situation where you are a young mother who now has to take care of all the finances and the running of the family home after your spouse dies? If your partner didn't have a life policy or leave you money you could find yourself with financial problems, which are likely to add to any insecurities. It can feel overwhelming, but there are things you can do to cut costs and maybe earn more. If you are not working, check with your local benefits section of the Job Centre to see what claims you might be eligible for. It might help to remind yourself that you are a resourceful person. Think of all the things you have managed to achieve in your life to date and draw on that. Tell yourself that you will manage again, that you will get through this, and you will.

Q: I have been left in a lot of debt. What can I do?

A. Try the UK *Consumer Credit Counselling Service* (CCCS) on 0800 1381111. They will go through your financial incomings and outgoings to assess your situation. They can negotiate a realistic repayment scheme between you and your creditors to help you pay off your debts. (Be careful not to confuse services like the CCCS, which offers advice and guidance only, with finance companies that take over your debt and add interest fees). Turn over management of debts to a competent person.

My husband died of cancer seven years after we married. We had two young children and we had struggled financially. After he died I was virtually penniless and had to start again. It was hard for a while but I did manage to build a life for our children and myself. I trained through a Job Centre initiative and got a job as a result. At first I leant heavily on friends and family but as time went on I became more independent.

Jane

Q. I've heard there's something called a Bereavement Allowance. Can you tell me about this and any other benefits I might claim?

A. In the UK, Bereavement Allowance is paid for a maximum period of 52 weeks after the death. The claimant must be over 45 years of age and not retired. Alternatively, if you are a parent and claiming child benefit you might be eligible for a Widowed Parent's Allowance (Bereavement Allowance and A Widowed Parent's allowance can't be claimed at the same time). A Widowed Parent's Allowance can also be claimed if you are pregnant with the deceased's child. You might be eligible for a one-off Bereavement Payment (currently £2,000 – this must be collected within 12 months) if your partner paid the required amount of National Insurance contributions and you are under retirement age. To find out more about these and any other claimable benefits, contact your local Benefits office.

Things to consider that may help ease your financial situation include:

- If you own your house, downsizing or moving to a cheaper area (longer term plan).

- Changing the mortgage to interest only for a while.

- Making savings on your outgoings.

- Considering taking a job (full or part time) if you are presently unemployed.

- Working from home.

- Sorting out childcare.

- Cashing in any assets.

Becoming a widow or widower

If you and the deceased were together for many years you are likely to have had shared memories, family and friends and a way of life. You probably knew each other inside out, knew each other's habits and possibly, like most of us, took each other for granted. But when your partner died you perhaps realized how intertwined your lives were and for a while you might feel totally at a loss without them. Life can change dramatically after the death of a spouse. The daily rituals you have shared, perhaps for a lifetime, have gone.

You probably had your own roles within the relationship; they might have been traditional roles or they might have been different but, over the years, you will have established routines and patterns.

Ruby died a couple of years ago and when she went I didn't know what to do with myself. We had this routine, since I retired. I'd go to the shop for Ruby first thing, while she hoovered and dusted round. I would get the paper and a few groceries and we would have some breakfast when I got back. Then in the afternoon we would take the dog down the park or I would do some gardening or fix something – Ruby always had something that needed fixing. But when she died, all that went. All of a sudden our routines had gone.

John

People sometimes say that their status in society changed when they became single again. They felt 'extra' in many social situations. Holidays and weekends can be the most difficult, when couples usually spend time together. You can be left feeling that there is all the time in the world and you have nothing to fill the space. However, although it might feel hard to believe now, it is possible to lead a busy social life as a single person. Just as you needed to make adjustment when you first became part of a partnership, it will also take time to adjust to being single. At first the companionship of friends might not seem as fulfilling as sharing the intimacy you had with a partner, but try not to compare the two and give yourself time to adjust and enjoy the company of friends.

Instead of sitting at home feeling lonely why not try contacting friends or someone from your family you haven't seen for a while? Don't forget that there are usually plenty of things to do locally. They might like to go with you to see a film, a play or an exhibition at a museum or perhaps try out the food in different local restaurants. Of course, you don't have to mix exclusively with single people, and if you want company keep in touch with friends who are couples, too. When you are feeling a bit stronger you might like to have a dinner party where you can invite a mix of people. Also, don't forget joining clubs or classes is a great way to meet new people with similar interests. You might not feel ready for these kinds of activities yet but keep them in mind for when you do. Don't forget that gradually things are changing for you, and when things get difficult, see them as temporary. Do more of what helps you.

A phrase from Eastern spiritual teachings helped me when I was mourning. It was: 'All things must pass.' It made me think about how death is part of life and that we all pass away one day, and also no matter how bad I felt at the time, it reassured me that these feelings would pass and others would take their place. It also helped me to think that the person who had died was at peace.

Pat

Part 3:
Long-Term
Challenges and
Future Hopes

In Part 3 we will be looking at a time when you can perhaps think about the future and building a new life for yourself. Time is the great healer, and as time passes we gradually come to terms with the death of our loved ones and start to live a life recreated through perseverance, courage and hope. First we will look at what is likely to be happening at this later stage – the challenges you might face now, and in the longer term, and what difficulties might hinder your progress in moving on. We address the negative feelings that might still bother you and how you can best cope with them. Then we look at signs of recovery, strategies for difficult days and what we might expect in our relationships with other people. Finally, we give a guide to practical matters that might arise and how you might invest emotionally in the future. You will find reassurance, support and advice throughout.

10

Where you are now

It's now two years since my husband died. I've been through so much in this time. People don't understand how much your life changes and what a huge gap is left when your partner dies. But I can now say that I am proud of how I have coped. I think the experience made me stronger in many ways and it made me appreciate how much I love people like my family and friends. It made me determined to make the most of my own life. Our son is at university and our daughter is doing her A levels.

I am so proud of them – we have all managed to support and comfort each other (when we have each had our wobbly times, and there have been many). Other family members and friends were also fantastic. I don't feel ready for a new relationship but I have noticed that recently I have stopped thinking it is out of the question.

Connie

It might help at this stage to take stock of how you are feeling about things now. Perhaps you have begun to feel hope for the future, either tentatively or with enthusiasm. You have come a long way, and when you look back at the first acute stage of bereavement – the first few days, weeks and months – you are likely to see big changes in how you think and feel, and how you are coping generally. You have possibly had to make major adjustments after the loss of the person you were deeply connected with. Hopefully you can appreciate what you have achieved but it might also feel that there is still some way to go. You can be the judge – try to judge your achievements by your own yardstick and be proud of yourself. At this later stage of grief you have been through a lot; you have had to work at getting on with day-to-day living when you might have been in devastating emotional pain and now in this later stage of mourning you perhaps feel it is time to move on with your life (or at least stick your toes in the water).

It is still early days, possibly, in terms of what you can expect of yourself and those around you. Certainly the first year after bereavement is still a time of adjustment for most of us, especially if the person who died was a major love in our lives or if we were dependent on the person or if they were dependent on us. Our lives go through massive changes and we need to adjust on both emotional and practical levels.

You might not necessarily feel that you have completely come to terms with losing the person but perhaps you can see that how you feel has changed even further. Hopefully, you feel better physically, and have returned to regular sleeping and eating patterns (if not, refer to Part 5, Chapter 16 for help with this). Time gives us the opportunity to reflect on the deceased's life and the life we had together. Don't expect too much from yourself if you still feel very much affected by the loss, some people believe that it takes two years to fully grieve and reach recovery – others find that it takes even longer. Try to ignore the clock and trust in your own ability to heal. Give it the time you need and remember, there are no rights and wrongs, only what you feel, and whatever you feel is okay. Maybe you can tell that you have made headway and notice that there are shifts in your thoughts, emotions and behaviour. Don't forget that grief is a gradual process.

As we have seen, in the first stages of grieving we struggle with disbelief and have to face the reality of the death. Acceptance comes again at this later stage and what we now have to accept is the possibility of building a life again and making plans for the future. Gradually, we need to move on with our lives, let go of the person who has died, and begin a new life of our own. We might think, 'Where do we begin?' Well, in fact, we began soon after the death. Everything that you have felt, and have gone through, is preparation for your new life. You have worked hard at surviving your devastating loss. You have done brilliantly and you should tell yourself this every day.

Longer term challenges

From day one, grieving is a challenge. Getting through each day can seem a mammoth task, but things do start to get easier and eventually we reach a place where we feel increasingly able to take on more challenges. Again we need to stress that if you aren't ready at any time to try out new challenges then please don't feel that you are failing in any way. It simply means you are not ready yet – we are all different and we deal with things the best we can at the time. We can perhaps see the longer term challenges of grieving as:

- Returning to (what feels to you) a more normal life.

- Living without yearning for the person and without related emotional pain (most of the time).

- Building a new life and making plans for the future in a life without the person.

- Trusting in life and going forward without fear.

- Letting go of the person as they were in life and holding them in your thoughts and heart.

Holding on

Many of us believe that the person who died is with us at times of difficulty. There are many beliefs about what happens after death and you can continue to be reassured by what comforts you. When people miss their loved ones and yearn for contact with them, they sometimes consult a clairvoyant or medium. Some people swear by this type of help and they will tell you stories about how the deceased has, through the medium, told them things the medium couldn't have possibly known and how they gave them guidance and advice. Mostly people go to see clairvoyants because they want to be assured that their loved one is okay and because they want to be reunited with them in some way. If you are tempted to do this be aware that, if you start to rely on contacting the deceased through clairvoyance, and if it stops you forming other relationships and getting on with your life in the present, then it could be a hindrance – it could possibly hold you back. (Also be aware of the possible risk of charlatans and remember that you are vulnerable at the moment.)

Holding on to the memory of a loved one is surely a good thing – why should you ever forget them? We don't have to forget the person and we have our memories, but if we continue to live in a way that holds us back from living our life to the full in the present, and we are living in the past, it is perhaps not such a healthy thing. Perhaps it is understandable that those who are older, and who have had many years with a partner and feel that they haven't much time left themselves, are exceptions. However, for the majority of people, basing our lives around a loved one who has died isn't helpful. It can prevent us from investing our love and emotions into other relationships and from finding meaning in our lives in the present.

This doesn't mean that you should stop thinking about the person or doing things like lighting a candle for them (or other rituals) that make you feel closer to them, but it is important that you let other people in to share your life and that you try to do those things that enhance your life, that prove to you that life is still worth living. You deserve to be happy, healthy and to have enthusiasm for the future. Holding on too tight to your loved one could hold you back. It could stop you being open to a new love in your life or stop you doing things that you always wanted to and might now be free to do. Writing about his grief experiences after his wife's death from cancer,

C. S. Lewis wrote in *A Grief Observer*, 'As I have discovered, passionate grief does not link us with the dead but cuts us off from them.'

Some people believe that it is important for the deceased that we let go of them otherwise we might hinder their progress in the afterlife. The point is you are still alive and have some living to do. There are certain things that might be holding you back, such as:

- Negative thinking: 'I don't deserve to be happy', 'I don't deserve to be alive – it should have been me instead of them.'

- You are still punishing yourself.

- Guilty or angry feelings.

- Negative thoughts linked to the deceased.

- Fear – of now, the future, your own abilities, your ability to love again and your own mortality.

- Other people's opinions.

Letting go

We hear people say that at some point we need to 'let go' of our loved ones. If we loved and had a deep attachment to someone why would we want to let them go? Perhaps in a sense we need to and yet in another sense we don't, and we certainly shouldn't feel we have to let go of our loved ones before we are ready to. The sad truth is that they have gone from the physical world we know but it is perhaps heartening to think that we haven't lost them completely, because we carry them in our consciousness, in our hearts and minds.

Often, when people talk about letting go, what they mean is that we need to let go of the pain associated with the loss, and make the transition in our thoughts and emotions, from having the person with us in life and accepting that it is possible to build a life without them. Try not to listen to those who tell you what you should be feeling or doing and try to trust in your own judgement. You will know best. Grief has a way of telling us what is right for us at any given time and it is important that we listen to what our bodies and emotions tell us. We feel what we feel and we are gradually healed, there is no hurrying it.

11

Difficulties that might still affect you

In Part 2 we looked at some particular types of grief that have their own difficulties. These included death by violence, the death of a partner and the death of a child. Complicated grief can make it harder for you to let go of your loved one and build a life without them. Again, we would urge you to seek professional help or support from a relevant agency if the problems persist. But let's look at some of the possible reasons you might still be disturbed by the loss; and again at some of the situations that might prove to be particularly difficult or painful.

Losing a parent or grandparent

Sometimes it can feel that we not only lose the person we loved but also a part of our selves. In close relationships our identities are wrapped up with one another's and when the person dies it can temporarily feel as if we have lost our identity. When a parent, grandparent or someone else of an older generation from our family dies, we lose people who have known us all our lives – they knew us as children and watched us grow into adults. Perhaps they were a source of great kindness to us; perhaps we felt that they understood us and knew our characters inside out. When a parent dies we possibly lose the person who was there for us unconditionally and who loved us in a way that nobody else can.

Of course, this might not be the case. We might have had an uncaring or abusive parent (or other close relative) and yet still be heavily affected by their death. We might partly have felt glad or relieved that they died. In which case you might also suffer guilt. If you have never disclosed the abuse to anyone, you might also be carrying feelings of anger and shame. If this is true for you (and whether the abuser was a parent, a family member, a family associate or a partner or the abuse was physical, mental or sexual), it would probably benefit you to talk with a counsellor or contact a relevant helpline (see Part 5, Chapter 18).

Losing a partner

When our partners die, life can change drastically. We might miss their touch, the sound of their voice, their humour, their kindness and all sorts of things that made them who they were and what they were to us. We are likely to miss them dreadfully because our lives were so much connected with theirs. We are likely to miss them on a practical day-to-day level as well as on an intimate level. We might find ourselves getting two coffee cups out, only to realize we need just the one. All the plans we made together change and we might find ourselves in circumstances that are considerably more difficult than before. We might feel like we have lost a soul partner; we might miss having a sexual relationship and it might be the case that they knew us when we were younger and perhaps more vibrant.

If we are older, then we might feel totally lost and disorientated – we might never have paid a

---

Q: What support is there for older people?

A: Contact *Help the Aged*, *Age Concern* and Social Services in the UK who can tell you about their services and point you in the direction of other helpful agencies.

---

bill in our adult life and we might have to take over all the practical things of life without much help. (Don't forget to contact the Benefits Agency through your local Job Centre to check what, if any, benefits you qualify for and Social Services – you will find their telephone numbers in Yellow Pages.) **Above all, give yourself time to grieve and adjust to the changes your loss has brought about.**

The aftermath of losing a child

When we lose a beloved child it can feel like our heart and spirit is broken. (Remember, the child can be any age and whether they were 1 or 41, when they died, it is likely to strongly affect us.) It goes completely against the grain when a young child dies; our instincts tell us to protect, love and watch over them and that is all cruelly taken away. It can be harrowing. We have to let go of all our hopes and aspirations for them – all their potential as a person and of our relationship with them. It is understandable if we feel angry or directionless for a while. It is also understandable that we might have regrets. We might think, 'If only we had taken that holiday instead of saving the money', 'I should have bought him those expensive football boots he wanted', 'I shouldn't have argued with her the week before she died.' Remorse and regret are natural parts of the grieving process but these kinds of thoughts can make it harder to let go. Please don't beat yourself up. You did your best in your relationship with the person when they were alive and you are doing your best now to survive the loss and carry on. Hopefully you have good memories, too, that perhaps outshine the problems you had in the relationship.

It is natural that at times we feel resentful that a terrible thing has happened to us. We might, at certain difficult times in the future, still feel 'Why did this happen to me – what did I do to deserve this?' We are not saints. Sometimes we will lash out in some way, a sense of injustice biting at us, so try not to be too hard on yourself if this happens to you. If you feel that life has dealt you a terrible blow, occasionally you will be caught off guard in your emotions. However, if you constantly still have strong feelings of anger or guilt that continue to affect your life then get some help. You might like to refer to page 206 and look at the list of reasons you might benefit from seeing a bereavement counsellor. It could be that you felt that you could struggle on alone but please don't. Getting help after bereavement is sensible. You owe it to yourself to have as good and full a life as you possibly can – you really do – so if strong emotions are still ruining your enjoyment of life then please get some help.

> *My son died when he was 21.*
> *Sometimes when I hear other women*
> *talking about their sons, and how*
> *they're getting on, I suddenly feel quite*
> *angry and spiteful and I have to get*
> *away. I feel that they're being smug –*
> *they've got their son and I haven't.*
> *I know they're not really being smug or*
> *mean to be unkind and feelings like this*
> *don't last long. I don't bear any grudges*
> *towards the women and I'm happy for*
> *them that they still have their sons, but*
> *it brings it back sharply that I haven't*
> *got mine.*
>
> **Heather**

> **MYTH:** *People are over a death after a year or so, and it causes more harm than good to mention the deceased to them.*
>
> **FACT:** Again and again it needs emphasizing, there are no time restrictions to grieving. People grieve in their own time. Talking about the deceased helps people to accept the death, get through the pain and then, ultimately, to move on.

Coping with horrible images

When you think of the person, try to see them as happy and at peace. If they died in violent or difficult circumstances this is likely to be harder for you, because you might have a 'bad' picture come into your mind at times relating to how you imagined they died. This is particularly difficult to cope with and we can feel haunted by such images and it can make us feel ill or even that we are going mad. Please remind yourself that your loved one isn't in pain or suffering any longer. It might also be comforting to remind yourself that when we are badly hurt we don't feel pain at the time – our bodies go into shock and it prevents us from registering the pain.

If you do have any disturbing pictures coming into your mind try to replace these with different, happier images. You could try a simple visualization exercise: Picture the person happy and smiling, see them in a place they loved to be while they were alive, or you could picture them in a beautiful heaven-like setting. Try to visualize using all your senses. If you see the person in a beautiful garden then hear the birds, see the butterflies and smell the beautiful lush flowers. Picture your loved one relaxed and at peace and perhaps smiling at you, telling you everything is all right.

It can help to have a strategy ready for difficult thoughts. This might be tapping either your chin or the back of your hand to remind yourself of what you are thinking and to break the focus. Do this, and as you tap, replace the image that hurts you with an image that consoles you. Or you might like to visualize the difficult image getting smaller and smaller until it disappears and then try to replace it with a more comforting image. (You'll find further calming relaxation strategies to help with panicky feelings in Part 5, Chapter 16.)

Persistent anger

Perhaps you still hold a lot of anger (maybe not all the time, but underneath your struggles to get on with life, anger and frustration might bubble away). Maybe you feel that life has dealt you a huge injustice and that what happened to you is unfair and cruel – and that is probably true. But it would be a terrible shame, and a waste of your life, to let it eat away at you. Perhaps you feel anger towards someone who was responsible for the death of your loved one. In reality, this might be a drunk driver or a murderer and in circumstances like these, anger is justifiable. A terrible, shocking thing has happened to you. However, the problem is, even though anger might have initially made you feel a bit better (there was someone to lash out at, and it is often said that we can't grieve and be angry at the same time), in time it might make you feel worse and ruin your chance of happiness. Forgiveness can be liberating.

Of course you don't have to forgive (the circumstances might feel unforgivable) and if you choose not to, it might help you to say this clearly to yourself and then put your energies into something positive like setting up a fund or charity in the deceased's name or taking legal action or campaigning for a change in the law. This will give the benefit of feeling that you are doing something and this can be a comfort.

If you are troubled with persistent anger it might help to think about who it is you are angry with. It could be:

- The person who caused the death – this can be real or imagined, for instance you might believe a doctor was negligent when they did all they could.

- The person who died – commonly felt in the case of suicide.

- Other people – who perhaps you feel don't understand (You think things like 'She still has her daughter').

- Life – 'Why did this happen to me?'

- God – loss of faith, no longer seeing religion as a source of comfort.

- Yourself – you could have thoughts like: 'I should have…' 'I could have…' 'If only I'd…' 'I let him/her down.'

All of the aforementioned are understandable targets of anger. Depending on the circumstances it might be reasonable to blame the person who caused the death. As we have seen in the case of suicide, it is understandable that we feel angry that the person has left us by taking their own life. Naturally we are likely to feel angry at life for being so cruel and uncaring to our loved ones, and us, and we might rail against God (if we are of a religious persuasion and sometimes even when we are not) but often we think that it is God or the universe we are angry with and in fact underneath it all we are angry (unreasonably) with ourselves. We think and feel things like 'I should have been there...' 'If only I had picked her up from the nightclub myself.'

We might blame ourselves relentlessly and we can, if we are not careful, literally worry ourselves to death. If it is yourself that you are angry with, then please try to let go of your anger. You will know if you are angry with yourself if, in your mind, you are saying things like 'I'll never forgive myself...' and it might help you to clarify what exactly you won't forgive yourself for. (It may be best to enlist the help of a counsellor or therapist to do this.) It might be that you shouted angry words at your daughter the day before she killed herself. It might be that you felt that you encouraged your son to join the army and when he was killed you blamed yourself. These kinds of situations are incredibly painful and it is more than understandable that you want to blame yourself but the truth is that the cause of death and the situations that led to them are complicated and it is unreasonably hard for you to take the blame on your shoulders.

Your loved one would, more likely than not, hate it that you are punishing yourself. Of course they would like you to have loving, happy memories of them and of the time you had together and they would like you to get on with your life in as positive a way as you can. Also, think about it, if it were you who died, would you want those left behind to suffer, or their life to be diminished in any way? If you think you were at fault in some way, try to forgive yourself. Sometimes when we carry blame, it stops us from truly being in touch with our feelings and talking to a professional might help you find some release. Whether you can forgive others is a matter for your own conscience. It isn't a case of whether it is right or wrong to forgive but when we do find it in our hearts to forgive (even that which seems unforgivable), we are likely to be more at peace.

Q: What support is there for the families of soldiers who die in combat?

A: Contact the *War Widow's Association of Great Britain* (whose aim is to improve the conditions of the lives of war widows, widowers and dependants), and the *Army Widows Association* (which offers bereavement support to widows, widowers and dependants). For further help and support, see details for the *Soldiers, Sailors, Airmen and Families Association (SSAFA)* in Part 5.

My son was in the armed forces and was stationed abroad. I was frightened for his life every day he was there. And then my greatest fears came true. His vehicle was ambushed and he was killed. He was 28 and had a wife and child. It was hard, but eventually I found it in my heart to forgive the person(s) involved, even though he had a brutal death. What good would it do me to carry hate in my heart? – that would be letting them destroy me and my family's life too.

Evelyn

Does fear hold you back?

Some days you might like to shut yourself away and curl up in bed or on the sofa and there really isn't anything wrong with that – as long as it is for no longer than a day or two – but it could mean that there is something you are avoiding. It could be a reluctance to do things you need to do or it could be that you are feeling afraid. After a major death in our lives things are often drastically different. We can lose track of our lives and it is not uncommon for people to become afraid. People sometimes call it 'losing the plot' and this isn't a bad description of what can happen to us after bereavement. Our lives are going along nicely; we have a plot (routines, hopes, plans for the future) and then wham! – there are sudden diversions from all we know. It is little wonder that we can lose trust in life for a while.

Sometimes we don't know what we are afraid of but fear lurks in the background for some time. It could be a fear of our own mortality following the death of someone close; if we were the same age as the person who died or if the person died of a hereditary illness, or if they shared a similar lifestyle to ours, like smoking and drinking excessively or are overweight. If thoughts like these are troubling you then see your GP and get checked out and resolve to improve your health.

If the death was particularly shocking (came out of the blue or a violent death) it is understandable to feel afraid and find it hard to trust in life for a while – you might feel afraid of what life holds for you in the future. Perhaps you fear that you will be alone or that you will die suddenly yourself. Life can feel precarious. If things have become more difficult for you in a practical or financial way then this could add to fears about the future. You might have thoughts that start 'What will I do if…?' or 'How can I…?'

There is a saying 'Feel the fear and do it anyway' and it is sound advice. 'Doing it' might mean just carry on living. Be careful of thinking too far into the future, it can make you afraid. It is best to deal with things day by day, step by step, and try not to worry about the rest. Maybe you could set yourself small challenges. It is natural and understandable to fear what the future holds when we have been painfully bereaved but, when we face our fears, then whatever we were frightened of usually disappears. It might help you to think that difficult feelings are temporary and they will pass.

We are all frightened of trying new and

challenging things and there is no bigger challenge than moving forward in our life after bereavement. Don't let fear stop you getting on with your life. Perhaps you can tell yourself that you deserve a good life and that you are a strong resilient person. Try using the affirmation cards again (written on business-size card and easy to carry around in your purse or wallet). You might try writing something like: 'I trust in life, I'm not afraid' or something encouraging like 'I can do it!'

Before my dad died I was very confident and happy but after he died I couldn't cope with how I felt. I really changed – I had this niggling fear of everything – I gave up playing sports, started drinking at home and didn't go out much. After a close friend told me that he was really worried about me I decided to go to counselling and it was a great help. I feel I'm back on track.

Adam

Thoughts about what happens to us when we die

Sometimes the fear we feel is a fear of death in general. If you think this is true for you it could be helpful to think about what you believe happens to us when we die. Some people have spoken about 'near death' experiences when they 'died' for a few moments (perhaps in an operating theatre) and they have often said things like they saw a blinding white light; some talk about going through a tunnel and going into bright white light and many talk about being met by a deceased person or persons they love. Images like these are reassuring to many people because they feel that their loved ones are in a beautiful and caring place with those they love who have also 'passed over', and that death is not so frightening. It can feel like those who died were here one minute and gone the next or they were somehow whisked away from us, and our beliefs might give us reassurance.

As we have seen, many people take comfort in religious ideas like heaven, angels and reincarnation. Ideas like these give us hope that the person is not completely gone altogether and that they go on to live on another plane. Don't forget to continue taking comfort from your beliefs about death. You might not place your beliefs in a religious context but instead think things like 'She's in a better place'. You might believe in angels (without necessarily believing other religious ideas) and that they are looking after your loved one.

Of course, not everyone has beliefs like these. Some people believe that we live and then die and that is reality. So what can comfort you if this is what you believe? One thing you must remind yourself of is that after we die (and this doesn't go against your beliefs) we are no longer in pain or suffering in any way. If you believe that the physical body is all there is, and after it is gone nothing of the person exists, do hold on to the fact that what does remain is the love you feel for the deceased. Human love and its effects can't be denied. Be comforted by the love you shared with the person who died because it is still with you and always will be. It is in your heart and in your thoughts and love cannot be destroyed by death.

Love is tangible – we feel it in our bodies. It can make us feel good to feel love for another person and love remains with you. Perhaps thoughts like these can be a comfort to you.

MYTH: *In time we will forget what the person who died looked liked.*

FACT: This is very unlikely unless we develop Alzheimer's disease or dementia and even then, we might not lose our memories of people who have died. We do sometimes, shortly after the death, think (or worry) that we are losing the memory of what the person looked like but this is usually to do with shock. If children are very young when the person dies they might not remember what the person looked like, but photographs can remind them.

Complicated grief symptoms

Hopefully you have some hope for the future and are taking tentative (or bold!) steps towards introducing new things into your life, although this doesn't mean that you don't have worries or concerns. You are human and you are bound to have doubts at times about how you will manage in the future.

If you have financial or practical difficulties you might continue at times to feel exasperated with the deceased, 'How could you leave me to just get on with everything?' Alternatively, you might have recurring feelings of guilt, 'If only I was there when she died' or 'If only I could have protected her.' Grief symptoms can become problematic when they persist for a long time and make us either very stressed or unhappy.

Here is a list of some of the complicated grief symptoms you might be feeling now. Tick any that apply to you:

❑ You can't get certain things out of your head.

❑ You constantly feel guilty.

❑ You constantly feel angry (at yourself, others/the deceased).

❑ You feel little hope for the future.

❑ You have cut yourself off from friends.

❑ Your sleeping pattern is erratic.

❑ You still have mood swings.

❑ You feel exhausted.

❑ You are not interested in sex.

If you have ticked more than one or two of the above then see your GP and talk to them about counselling or psychotherapy.

12

The signs of recovery

We talk about 'getting over' or 'getting through' a painful bereavement. Grieving can feel like we are being stretched to the limits of our endurance. At its worst, it can feel like a wall of darkness and something we will never get over; it can also feel like we go somewhere in our minds that is impenetrable to other people – we feel they can never understand. We can feel like we are going mad because of the strong and sometimes overpowering emotions we have. Nevertheless, somehow, we do manage to get through those terrible days, weeks and months of early bereavement and things gradually change for the better. We begin to recover.

How can we tell when we are on the mend? What are the signs that our hearts and spirits are healing and things are changing for the better? For some it might mean that they don't cry so often, for others it might mean that they begin to

---

Signs of recovery might include:

- Feeling enjoyment and enthusiasm again.

- Becoming more aware of your love for other people/appreciating them.

- Becoming more aware of your surroundings.

- Making plans.

- Recognizing your strengths and achievements.

- Feeling lighter in yourself.

- Taking care of yourself.

- Planning for the future.

- Feeling hope for the future.

enjoy doing things again and perhaps that they no longer think about the deceased all the time. We might begin to socialize again, want to decorate our homes or find ourselves laughing heartily for the first time in ages. It is important that you let yourself recover in your own time and if and when you sense things improving for you, let yourself enjoy it.

Strategies for dealing with difficult times

Anniversaries can be particularly hard to cope with, as they can bring into focus the life we shared with the deceased. The fact they are not with us anymore is highlighted at these times. Anniversaries normally represent happy times and when we think about them we might naturally once more yearn to be with the deceased. We might say to ourselves things like, 'We would have been married 20 years today' or 'Kevin would have been 18 today.' Birthdays and Christmas are also tricky dates on the calendar and you might long to spend time with your loved one. Another difficult time is the anniversary of the person's death. It is not uncommon for people to say that they have noticed they feel unwell around this time, as if their body is programmed to feel the anguish they were going through at the time.

It will help you if you can build some strategies for difficult times. Some people prefer to distract themselves on meaningful dates and others find a way to make them meaningful.

For the first year I dreaded holidays, like bank holidays and the summer holidays, when the kids were off school for weeks on end. I felt so lonely. My parents were great – the first summer around the anniversary of Tim's death, they took us all off to Cornwall for a break and we actually had fun but it would hit me at night when the kids had gone to bed. My mum and I would sit up talking to the early hours and I would weep and feel a bit better. I now have a network of friends and am hardly ever stuck for company when I need it.

Carol

It might help you cope if you:

- Give yourself a treat on the day – a facial, a swim, a meal with a friend, a game of golf.

- Do something unusual, something you don't normally do – see a show, or take a trip somewhere different.

- Make contact with another person who was close to the deceased and whose company you enjoy.

- Visit a place that was special to you and the deceased.

- Have a family gathering – perhaps with a meal or drinks.

- Take flowers to the grave, light a candle, look at photos or refer to the memory box/book.

At every stage of grieving you can expect to have low moments or even low days. And the reality is, that if the person who died was someone who you loved very much (and perhaps this is most true when we lose a child), this could happen for the rest of your life. Some people say things like 'I've thought of them every day of my life' or 'They are the first thing I think about when I wake up and they are the last thing I think about before I go to sleep', when they have lost someone dear to them many years before. Please don't be alarmed by this because all it means is that you will never stop loving them and also remember that the emotions will never again be as hard to manage as they were at first. Hopefully, you have noticed by now, from your own experience, that emotions and their effects change with time.

Whereas, at first, your emotions might have been so strong that it perhaps made you physically weak and you felt completely overwhelmed by them, you will feel more and more at peace with the loss as time goes by. It is the difference between feeling waves of sadness and needing to cry, and feeling that your heart has been wrenched from your chest as you perhaps did in the early days – remember all those unmanageable feelings, and how your body reacted. Of course you will still feel sad at times, it is only natural.

People often describe how they feel as having 'waves of emotion'. Sometimes, you might still suddenly feel engulfed by a big wave – maybe when something suddenly reminds you of the person, like hearing a song or seeing other people's children grow and develop or being at one of your children's schools at prize-giving without your husband. Don't be alarmed, it doesn't mean that you are not healing or things aren't improving, it just means that you had a sense of the person again and you were reminded of the love you have for them and what you miss about them.

Situations that might stir your emotions include:

- Anniversaries, birthdays and Christmas.

- Holiday times.

- Meeting people who don't know about the death.

- Hearing people talk about their child, friend, parent or partner.

- Being reminded of the person suddenly and poignantly.

- When you feel alone/loneliness.

When the stark reality of the death hits you once more, keep telling yourself that it is okay to be upset at times. Try to accept your feelings as natural and understandable.

You could keep a diary or lists of what you have found helpful so far – and don't forget to list positive developments. Seeing your achievements (big or small) in written form can spur you on. Perhaps you could pin them where you will see them often. These might include things like:

- I went out for a meal with work colleagues and managed it well.

- I met Lucy in the street and I felt fine when she mentioned that she and her husband were going on holiday together.

- I joined an art class and I'm enjoying it.

- Jenny and I painted my bedroom and it felt good to make changes.

- I had a haircut and a facial and felt good.

You have probably identified some things that have helped you before, so try these again. Have some strategies ready for low days. Taking a walk or another form of exercise will help, because exercise makes us more optimistic and relaxed. Many people like to talk to the deceased (either out loud or in their head) or go to a church and light candles or pray. Remember, you don't have to be religious to find comfort in these things – you could have some rituals of your own, like lighting candles at home or visiting a place you both loved.

Alternatively, you might like to turn to a memory box or book if you have made those and look at the photographs and other things you have stored there. Don't forget, you can send your loving thoughts to the person, or let yourself cry or shout (preferably in a place that doesn't disturb other people), or write your thoughts down. It can be very therapeutic to write your feelings down, either in a journal, diary or in letters to or about your loved one. You can read these at any time and, when you do, you will see all the different emotions you have gone through and how differently you feel at different stages of your grief.

Writing letters to your loved one or keeping a record of your thoughts and emotions (you can keep them in a box or special place) can help on different levels:

- It gives you an outlet for your thoughts and emotions.

- It can make you more aware of your thoughts and feelings.

- It can make you feel you have a link to the deceased.

- You can say things you would have liked to have said to the person but, possibly, didn't have the chance, such as: 'I'm sorry I couldn't...', 'I love you and appreciate all you did for me', 'I am angry that...', 'Thank you for...', 'I miss you dreadfully.'

- You can read them later and see how things have changed.

- And perhaps, if and when you're ready, you can write to say goodbye.

The importance of support networks

It is important that you have an ongoing network of support. It is important for all of us, but when we have been recently bereaved it is even more crucial. We need support while we take on new challenges and acclimatize to changes. Hopefully, you are still getting love and support from others and if this has dwindled then perhaps you could gently remind those close to you that you could, at least from time to time, do with some support and comfort. Sometimes just seeing someone and receiving a hug is enough. Not all of us have a large network of family and friends, some of us have invested a lot of our time and energies into a partnership or immediate family, and if you have let friendships and family contacts slip, then maybe you could consider contacting old friends or family members. Perhaps your religious community is a potential source of social contact and comfort. You might also like to join a local support group.

Have those around you forgotten?

As we have already seen, after a short time, support can ease off. Initially, people were anxious to see that you were all right and you had emotional and practical help but, after a while, you might have found that this kind of help diminished and people perhaps expected you to have moved on with your life. It would be understandable if you feel bewildered and you might ask yourself, in response, things like 'Why are they carrying on as if nothing has happened? They never mention Harry anymore, how could they?' or 'Don't they realize what I have been through?' and this might lead to angry feelings of rejection.

To be fair, if you're grieving for someone dear to you, then some of the other people around you might not have been so deeply affected by the death and might not truly understand what you have been going through. However, although your feelings might be less acute and debilitating than they once were, you might still need emotional support. You might be coping with the practical side of things but need to feel that other people, close friends and family at least, understand how you are feeling. Sadly, through no one's fault, they might not be able to give you what you need and, if this is the case, it would be good for you to find other sources of emotional and practical support. Support could come from other people who were close to the deceased (and who might be going through similar things to you) or another source altogether, for example, help agencies and support groups.

Other sources of support

Many charities offer support groups or mentor type support. Group members have usually had similar experiences, which might be the same type of death (like the death of a child or by suicide or through drugs). *The Compassionate Friends* (UK national telephone helpline: 0845 1232304), for instance, offers support and friendship for bereaved parents and their families by those who have been similarly bereaved. It can help tremendously to talk with those who have lost their loved ones in similar circumstances because you are likely to feel that they understand. You can talk freely about feelings and pent up emotions, such as anger or guilt, that you perhaps feel you need to protect others from.

Groups like these often offer practical support, too, so if friends or members of family are less affected by the death, then try not to be too harsh on them, and get other support elsewhere.

Continuing to talk about the person

You might have to remind people (yet again) that it is okay with you if they talk about the deceased. They might think that it isn't and that they will open wounds by doing so. However, when they don't it can feel as if they are acting as if the person – your beloved husband, child, parent or friend – never existed. They might seem to ignore major events, such as the person's birthday or your anniversary, and don't realize that sending you a card or calling on you would be comforting. People might think that you seem happier and more able to cope and think you will get upset again if they remind you of the deceased. You could try telling them how you feel and where you are with your grieving at the time.

If you talk about the person freely yourself, then others are likely to follow. Sometimes when other people talk about their family or friends, something they say might sound uncaring or insensitive and you might find yourself feeling angry or wounded. It may appear that they 'go on' about their spouse or child as if they are oblivious to your loss but they are probably trying to carry on as before, hoping that you are fine with what they are saying. We can't always know what people are thinking and doing and it is probably best to try to think their intentions are good.

Other people's advice

At this later stage of grieving, we might need to reassess the value of other people's advice. Other people are usually immensely supportive when they see that we are grief stricken. They often take over to try to alleviate our burden. They can be unselfish in their time and efforts and can show incredible kindness and we are usually very grateful. However, if a person is on the bossy or controlling side (and characters like this like to be useful!) they can take over a bit and, while their advice and support might have been incredibly helpful in the early stages, it might become a bit of a pain later.

It may be that they continue to advise you on what would be best for you or the children and you might begin to wish that you hadn't had to lean on them in the first place. However, no need to panic, all you need to do is thank the person profusely for their help to date and tell them what a great help they have been (which is probably true) and assure them that you are now able to take over and make decisions for yourself. Don't assume other people know best – it is you who are the expert of your own and your immediate family's emotions and needs.

MYTH: Counselling is very expensive – I wouldn't be able to afford it.

FACT: Counselling can be expensive when you see a counsellor privately, depending on location and how experienced and qualified the counsellor is. It can cost between about £20 and £60 per session. However, there are agencies like Cruse who offer free bereavement counselling and some counsellors offer concessions. Counselling over the internet can be a cheaper method of accessing counselling.

13

New relationships

Investing emotionally in the future

In time you will find that hope grows and you will be able to emotionally invest in the future. This could involve investing in new friendships and perhaps a new relationship. You might find that you are beginning to be open to the idea of meeting someone special or you might have already met someone and you are seeing new possibilities. Remember, finding happiness in a new relationship doesn't in any way negate the relationship you had with the deceased. No one can replace a loved one. You wouldn't want them to. You will still have the memories and love for the person who died – you don't need to give these up, but you might also have love to invest in a new relationship. Your thoughts and what you feel in your heart are private and no subsequent relationship needs to impinge on your feelings for the deceased.

When you were first bereaved the thought of finding love again might have seemed anathema, but now perhaps the idea has more appeal. You might miss the intimacy of a close relationship as well as the companionship. Perhaps you miss sharing your life as part of a couple, having meals, going out, and holidaying together.

You might wonder how you will know when you are ready to enter into a new partnership. This is difficult to answer, but you will know. If you are lucky it might happen naturally. You might meet someone out of the blue – although it has to be said that it does seem to get harder the older we get because we might not socialize as much as we did when we were younger and we don't have so many ways to meet people.

Perhaps you will decide to join a dating agency or agree to a blind date set up by a friend or agree to go to a dinner party knowing that a friend has matchmaking ideas. Of course, loneliness is the reason many of us seek out new partners – the home can become a lonely place – but it is not always the best of reasons because, out of fairness to ourselves and prospective partners, we need to have come to terms with the death of our ex-partner before we can invest in a new relationship. If we dive in at the deep end, before we are ready, then it could bring more heartache. We might unfairly compare the new person with the love we lost. If the relationship doesn't work out then it might spoil our confidence to date anyone else for a while.

To meet people of both sexes and develop friendships try joining organizations such as *The National Council for the Divorced and Separated* (for details see Part 5) where widows and widowers are welcomed to their social events.

Being realistic about the relationship you had with the deceased

There is a possibility that you might forever compare people you meet with the one who has died and it could be useful to ask yourself if you are being realistic about them. You wouldn't be unusual if you thought about your loved one in rosy terms only – remembering their good points, perhaps their thoughtfulness or level headedness (and ironically we might not have appreciated the good points fully when the person was alive) and seeing them as having had no faults. Yet we all have faults, so they must have had them too. Maybe you could sit with pen and paper and write a list of 'good' and 'not so good' aspects of the person's character and also what was 'good' and 'not so good' about your relationship. For instance, we might, in hindsight, give the person a sainthood in our minds for their kindness but when they were alive it irritated us that they spent so much time helping other people when perhaps we needed more of their attention. You won't be disloyal or cruel in any way by being realistic, and it could open the doors a teeny bit for other mere mortals to share your love in the present.

MYTH: There is no point in looking for anyone else – my wife was the love of my life.

FACT: If you are ready there is every point to dating. You could meet someone and find happiness together. Your wife might feel like the love of your life, and she will always remain special to you, but remember your life isn't over yet so let yourself find happiness again.

You might be ready to find a new partner if:

- The right amount of time (for you) has passed and you are not trying to replace the person who has died.

- You feel more emotionally stable.

- You are no longer yearning for the deceased all the time.

- You can think of the deceased in realistic terms.

- You believe that you are ready to move forward in your life.

- Your libido has returned.

- You can imagine making a life with someone else.

There are many good reasons for entering into a new relationship again, not least having someone special to share your life with, and all that goes with that, including sex and intimacy, companionship and help with day-to-day living.

However, it is probably not a good idea to look for another partner because you would like to improve your finances or because you miss sex and intimacy. Although these might be very important, beware of trying to find someone to fit a task – it is not likely to work. It is likely to be more constructive to look for the qualities you like in a partner, such as kindness, warmth, intelligence and a sense of humour and if they have similar tastes and lifestyles to you.

There are many ways of meeting people with similar interests. Here are just a few suggestions:

- Join a class – there are many day or evening classes on all kinds of subjects (you might like to try learning a foreign language).

- Learn a musical instrument.

- Exercise – long walks in the countryside (you could perhaps join a rambling club), horse riding, cycling or something more daring you haven't tried before such as scuba diving, skiing or paragliding.

- Write – using your experience – perhaps short stories or a novel.

- Run a group – associations such as the Guides or Scouts often need helpers, or join a support group (contact your local groups).

- Work for a charity.

- Travel – experience different cultures and exciting places.

- Do volunteer work – contact the *Samaritans, Citizens' Advice Bureau* or overseas work (VSO's website address is: **www.vso.org.uk**.

Making longer term plans

It might feel like the time is right to make longer term plans. At first you perhaps weren't in a fit state to make major decisions but now maybe you are ready to make some further life changing decisions, like moving house or taking a long trip. Remember, however, that as a rule it is best not to make any life changing decisions, such as moving home, marrying or moving in with a partner, in the first year after a major bereavement, when further big changes might be too much strain.

MYTH: I should move house. It is unhealthy to live in the same house that I lived in with my deceased husband – it's full of memories.

FACT: There are no hard and fast rules. Some people like to stay in the home they know (this is often true with older people) and are comforted by the familiarity, while other people feel that they need a fresh start somewhere else. Follow your intuition.

Make a list of possibilities for now and the future. They might include:

- Moving house.

- Finding a partner.

- Getting a pet.

- A change of career.

- Going on holiday or on a world trip.

- Changing your job.

- Starting a business.

- Studying.

- Socializing more.

Spend a little time thinking about what you would really like to do, and ask yourself what is stopping you or what steps you might take now to make it possible at a later date (for instance, you could begin studying for a qualification that will in the future allow you to change careers).

Helping other people

Perhaps you would like to help other people who have been bereaved in similar circumstances. Helping others can feel productive. It is good to feel useful and it perhaps puts what you have gone through to good use. Without knowing it you may well be a wealth of information and you are likely to understand what the people are going through more than most. Contributing positively to the welfare of other people can help us enormously. It can make us feel that the person who died didn't die in vain. It is also a wonderful way to help and be helped; by sharing your experiences you bring your experience and gained wisdom to others and at the same time your experiences and feelings are acknowledged. It can give a sense of value to your loss (when perhaps it is otherwise hard to see that any good could have come from it). It helps people enormously to feel that what they are going through is understood, and who better to offer support than someone else who has had a similar experience?

You might like to start a charity in the deceased's name. Sometimes it helps people enormously to *do* something after a death. This is especially true when their loved one has died in violent circumstances. By setting up a charitable trust or campaigning for new policies in the law they feel that they are doing something for the person who has died. Usually the aim of charities is to offer both emotional and practical support as well as information. Some parents, who have lost a child, have found comfort in setting up a fund to help other young people. Calling a trust after a person means that their name lives on. Charities such as *Edward's Trust* or *Winston's Wish* do fantastic work and are wonderful legacies (see Part 5, Chapter 18).

MYTH: I've always fancied doing a degree in literature but at 54 I'm far too old.

FACT: Being a mature student is very common these days, and many people who embark on degree courses are older than 54. Good luck!

MYTH: Dating agencies are only for the young.

FACT: Although there is evidence to suggest that it is mainly people in the 30–50 age range that use dating agencies and 'lonely hearts columns', both older and younger people also use them.

Looking after an elderly parent

If one of your parents has died you could be in the position of caring for the surviving parent who might be frail and who has mobility problems. They might find it hard to care for their house and garden and shop for themselves. Perhaps you find yourself doing more and more to help and if you have a family of your own, the extra work can be demanding and exhausting.

Don't despair – you certainly don't have to struggle on alone and there are many ways to get help. You might like to start with contacting your local Social Services and ask them for an assessment of your parent's needs. They might benefit from services like 'meals on wheels' and help in the home.

Also, your parent might be eligible for help with funding for building alterations if it will enable them to stay in their property. For instance, they might benefit from installing a downstairs loo, wheelchair facilities or a stair lift. If your relative can't afford to make changes, they might qualify for financial help from a local council renovation grant or disabled facilities grant. You, or they, could contact the local housing department to check what help is available. Some councils offer home repair assistance for smaller jobs that need doing, like draught proofing. Also, if your parent or relative receives benefits they might be eligible for a Community Care Grant. Check with your local benefits office and Council Housing Department. You could also contact voluntary agencies such as *Age Concern* and *Help the Aged* as a further source of support (see Part 5, Chapter 18).

Having a parent move in with you

You might consider having a surviving parent (or other elderly relative) move in with you. If you are considering a big move like this you will need to be realistic about how well you get on with each other. If you have existing problems in your relationship then the situation is unlikely to improve when you are in closer proximity on a daily basis and if you constantly have to do things for them. What might seem like a kindness could be a huge strain on everyone concerned. You could end up feeling very hard done by and resentful. It is difficult enough to care for someone you get on well with and whose company you enjoy, but impossible when there is a personality clash; for instance, if you find the person crabby or over critical this is likely to wear you down.

It might take some of the pressure off if, instead of living in the main part of the house, they have an annexe or space solely for their use. If you have a busy family life you will need to think about how it will work – noise, children's needs, visitors, cooking times etc. Incidentally, if your home requires conversion for your parent then any housing department grants will be assessed on their means, not yours as the householder.

If you become a full-time carer you could qualify for a carer's allowance. You can call your local benefit's agency to check. *Carers UK* (for details see Part 5) provides support and advice for carers, including finding respite care.

Sheltered housing

If your relative is in reasonably good health but is older and perhaps needs keeping an eye on, then sheltered accommodation could be an option they might like to consider. Sheltered housing is specially designed housing with warden attendance. The residents can contact the warden day or night in cases of emergencies. Each person has their own self-contained accommodation and there are often shared areas, such as gardens and sitting rooms. 'Very sheltered housing' and 'extra care' schemes offer extended services, for example, like help with personal care (bathing and dressing) or domestic help and meals.

Sheltered housing can be bought or part bought (where a housing association or local authority retains ownership of part of the property and rents out their part to the tenant) or rented. If your relative plans to buy this type of property bear in mind that there are likely to be services charges on top of the initial outlay.

Alternatively, a residential or nursing home might suit your relative's requirements best. Residential homes offer domestic and personal care without nursing. The nursing home provides a greater level of care and older people often move from a residential home to a nursing home if they need nursing. This might happen if a person develops dementia or Alzheimer's disease or becomes incontinent and generally needs closer attention and medical care. Ways to help your elderly parent or relative include:

- Helping them to stay in their own home.

- Having them move in with you.

- Helping them move to secure housing.

- Helping them move to a residential or nursing home.

- Checking that they are getting all the care/support they are entitled to.

Given the choice, the surviving parent/relative usually prefers to stay in their own home. They might like to remain in familiar surroundings where they feel independent and in control. Their homes are filled with memories and it can be another blow to lose the home shortly after the death of their partner. They often fear that they will 'be a bother' to their children. However, if they are frail in health and forgetful you might worry for their safety. If they are to stay in their own house there are a number of things that you could do to improve their safety and comfort. If you have concerns about the conditions your relative is living under, call local authorities such as the housing and grants departments to check what help they might get and Social Services to enquire about their provisions (you'll find their local telephone number in Yellow Pages).

Looking after yourself

Why not try to do things to make your life as hassle free and joyful as possible too? Try not to spend all your time looking after other people – make sure that you also have the best quality of life you can. Remind yourself there are many opportunities open to you. Perhaps try something you have always wanted to do or new things that have no association with the past.

Spiritual pursuits

Remember that to look after others, you first need to look after yourself. Doing creative things, for example, dancing, singing and artwork, can bring some joy back into your life. In Part 4 you will read heart-warming testimonies of other people who have survived difficult bereavements and have gone on to find life meaningful and enjoyable again and in Part 5 you will find relaxation exercises and many ways to look after yourself.

The world is a beautiful place and at times we all need to remind ourselves of what we have in our lives that we can be grateful for. This might include:

- Our love for other people who are still alive – family (old and young), friends and workmates.

- Other people's love for us.

- Our health.

- Our home.

- Our work.

- Our love of nature – plants and animals.

- Our love of travel.

- Our hobbies or pastimes – a love of art, books, TV programmes and the computer.

Some positives from the experience of bereavement

Perhaps in time you will feel that there has been some personal gain as well as loss. You are likely to know now what your priorities are and whose friendship and love you value. Some bonds will have been strengthened by the loss. In time you might find a new spontaneity and adventurousness in yourself. You have learnt the hard way that it is important to make the best of life and you are possibly determined to live life to the full in the present. Perhaps an enthusiasm for life is returning and you hold some hope for the future. There are still many great experiences waiting to happen. Time is precious.

Think of all the beauty still left around you and be happy.

Anne Frank

If my doctor told me I had only six minutes to live, I wouldn't brood. I'd type a little faster.

Isaac Asimov (writer)

Part 4:
Messages of Hope
and Support

14

From the postbag

Every letter sent to me at *This Morning* is confidential but these created letters are typical of the hundreds I receive.

Dear Denise

My husband died three years ago. We were married for 27 years and I thought at the time that I would never get over it. He was my world. Then about a year ago I met another man. He was very caring – asking how I had been coping and so on – and, although he had never been married he understood the bond I will always have with my husband. We started spending more time together. He has been very patient with me but I know he would like us to live together. The trouble is I just can't bring myself to do it. He makes me very happy and I care for him very much, but I feel as if I am betraying my husband by being with him. Sometimes I feel so guilty that I think about telling him I never want to see him again. Can you tell me what I should do?

Dear X

Thank you for your letter. I was so sorry to read about the difficulties you've been having. No one can replace your husband and you won't ever forget him but try not to see this other man as the problem. The problem is that you can't come to terms with the fact that you are still alive and have love to share, love that doesn't have to be taken away from your first love but will grow naturally as you let new people into your life. I think you really need to explore your own feelings and let go of grief. Doing that is not the same thing as letting go of your husband. Sometimes grief can get in the way of the old love so that we start to indulge the grief rather than celebrate the life we had with our loved one. I think you also need to work out how much you are motivated by fear of what other people might think. In the end, your own opinion of yourself is the only one that matters. You had a wonderful marriage. Nothing can ever alter that and a new relationship could be wonderful too. It sounds as though this new man is a very special person. Don't push him away because of a misplaced sense of loyalty. Everyone deserves a second chance at happiness, including you.

You may find it helps to talk things through with someone. Sometimes it takes a third party to help us make sense of our feelings and provide some guidance on where we might go from thereon. The *Family Contact Line* offer telephone counselling for anyone with a problem that needs discussing. It can be contacted on 0161 941 4011 on weekdays from 10 a.m. to 10 p.m. Similarly, *Marriage Care* offers listening support to anyone experiencing difficulties in their close personal relationships. The number is 0845 660 6000 and lines are open Monday to Friday from 10 a.m. to 4 p.m.

Dear Denise

I was 65 when I lost my dear wife to cancer four years ago. We had been married for 39 years and I was devastated. We had a good crowd of friends before my wife became ill and they rallied round. One of them was a widow and she and my wife were very close. After my wife died she helped me enormously just by letting me talk. It helped just letting things out to someone who knew what I was talking about. I suppose that's how we became close, we both knew what it was to love and lose. At the beginning we each talked about the love we had lost but gradually a new love began to grow. We were married a year and four months after my wife died. You may feel that this was too soon but my wife and I had often talked about how we wouldn't want the other one to be lonely if we went first. At the time it was just talk because you never think it will happen but I know she wouldn't have wanted me to be unhappy. She always wanted what was best for other people.

My wife has three children from her first marriage and grandchildren and I have a son and daughter. The wedding was a wonderful day with both families there but now my wife's children have become very distant. They believe that she took up with me far too quickly and feel that she has betrayed

their father's memory. They have been very cruel too,
saying things about their upbringing which have hurt
her very much and say they will never ever accept me
as part of their family. It is making us both unhappy
but it's worse for my wife. We are very happy
together and we can't understand why her children
feel the way that they do.

Dear X

I'm so sorry to read about the difficulties that
you and your wife are encountering with her
children and I certainly don't think your
marriage to each other commenced too quickly
after your wife's death. As far as I'm concerned
there is no 'date' on which it becomes acceptable.
You just know in your heart when it is right.
Finding happiness with someone else after the
death or departure of one's partner doesn't
negate the love that existed in that previous
relationship. You knew your first wife better
than anyone and know she would understand
and approve of your remarriage. Far from being
something to feel guilty about, your finding
happiness again should be celebrated. I think it's
wonderful that you have both been given a
second chance of happiness, but the fact that

such discord prevails amongst your wife's family must be deeply distressing and my heart goes out to you both.

It wouldn't be fair for me to speculate on why they have responded in this way without hearing the story from both sides. However, whatever the circumstances are I appreciate the hurt and bewilderment that you must both feel. Her children might be insisting that they want no further contact with their mother but it's also possible that bridges between all of you could be built in the future. It would be sad if she were to abandon hope of reconciliation with her children so I suggest you keep up contact with birthday and Christmas cards to grandchildren etc. It is still quite early days and it may simply be that the children need a little more time to adapt to this new situation. A lot will depend on their seeing that their father is still respected and loved and I know you will both make sure this is the case. I'd also suggest that your wife speaks to a sympathetic outsider about all of this. Talking things through with someone can bring a great deal of comfort, and may provide a clearer perspective on what has happened. *Parentline* operates a telephone counselling service for any parent under stress, and can be

contacted on 0808 800 2222 on weekdays from
9 a.m. to 6 p.m. I wish you both well and hope
you have many happy years together.

Dear Denise

*My son committed suicide two months ago and I still
can't believe it. He hanged himself and I found him. I
knew things had been hard for him recently but I
never imagined he would do this. I honestly didn't see
the signs and now I feel so guilty as I should have
known how unhappy he was and done something to
help. I am his mother. If he couldn't rely on me who
could he rely on? I don't know how to cope or what to
do. My heart is broken. Please help.*

Dear X

I was so sorry to read about your son's suicide.
You obviously cared deeply for him and to have
lost him in such a sudden and violent manner
must have been devastating. I can't even begin to
imagine the bewilderment and pain you must
feel, and perhaps anger too that he could leave
you in that way. I don't believe that anyone who
has a close, loving family or friends around them
would ever put them through this trauma unless
they had lost the ability to think through what
they were doing. At the point when they take
their own life I imagine that they believe that it
is the best or only thing they can do for either
themselves or the people around them. This
sense that they are a burden to others, seeing no
hope, and no way out of their situation suggests
to me that they were not thinking rationally at
the time they made that decision. I think we
must therefore forgive them for leaving us in
such a sudden and traumatic way.

It is not necessarily the case that everyone
who kills themselves is in the depths of
depression for a while beforehand. Sometimes
suicides aren't carefully planned but are a
momentary impulse. What is vitally important to

bear in mind is that there are often no visible clues that something is amiss. I know it is difficult to come to terms with that but I know from years of experience that to all intents and purposes the individual often appeared happy in his or her life, and never demonstrated any changes in personality or characteristics of being depressed. Sadly I have also learned over the years that if someone is determined to end their life, all the love in the world can't prevent it, but I realize that knowing this doesn't help to ease the pain of those left behind, grieving and wondering 'Why?'

What is imperative now is that you are supported. People deal with trauma in different ways and at different times, but if you can reach out for help you'll find enormous comfort. *Survivors of Bereavement by Suicide* (0870 241 3337 9 a.m. to 9 p.m. every day) provides emotional support and help to anyone who has lost a loved one through suicide. I would also recommend that you have a look at their website, **www.sobs.admin.care4free.net**) if you can as this provides some really useful advice. To find a local counselling service which offers one-to-one support, you can contact 01779 470163.

There have been times when I have lost people dear to me where I thought that my grief would overwhelm me. However, I somehow managed to get through those terrible days, until I found that some meaning had returned and I could start to believe that life could be worth living again. I'm sure that that is what your son would want for you.

Dear Denise

I am 23 years old and this will be the first year ever that I will be spending Christmas on my own. My husband was killed in a car crash just a few months after we got married. We had so many hopes and dreams and we didn't get a chance to make any of them come true. It is so hard to cope with what's going on around me. I hadn't really got used to being a wife and now I'm a widow. Even though I have the love and support of my family, and my in-laws, I still feel alone. I know I have to live out my life but sometimes I don't know how I can go on without my wonderful husband. Everybody around me seems to be full of the buzz of Christmas and I am dreading it. Please help.

Dear X

I was so terribly sorry to hear about your loss. That your husband was killed is absolutely tragic especially given the short length of time you had been married and to be widowed at 23 is something that no one should have to endure. It sounds as if you shared a very special relationship, and his absence will naturally have come as a terrible shock and left a huge void in your life. You won't ever forget him, but in time the hurt you feel now will diminish.

For the time being simply focus on getting through each day as best you can and I promise you that things will start to become easier. It is still very early days, and you certainly shouldn't feel that by now you should be coping better. Just as a physical wound will repair itself in its own good time, so an aching heart will take it's own time to ease. But it will ease and mend in time if you trust the process of grief and allow it to do its work.

I have lost both my parents, my only sister, my two former husbands and a much loved son and certainly there were many times when I thought that my grief would overwhelm me. But I somehow managed to get through those terrible days, until I found that some meaning had returned and I could start to believe that there were other things in the world that could make life seem worth living again. I have experienced great happiness in spite of loss and I know that this is possible for you, too. I'm sure that is what your husband would want for you. Grief cannot be defined in terms of time and there is an uphill journey in front of you now but I know that in honour of your husband and for your own sake, you will get through this.

As far as Christmas is concerned, there is no denying that it will be difficult. However, the important thing to remember is that it is only one day and you will get through it. You may want to devote some time to your husband whether it's on your own or with family. You may need a quiet moment to think about him, talk to him perhaps, or have a good cry. There is no reason to shut him out of Christmas. Remember how he loved it and the Christmases you spent together and if that makes you cry let the tears flow.

Eventually they will end and you will feel better for having released them. I do know that whether you feel him to be with you in spirit or not, he will be in your heart forever. Many people never find or experience such a love in their lives as you had and no one can ever take away that love or the wonderful memories you have of your husband.

The Widowed and Young Foundation (WAY) on 0870 011 3450 will understand exactly how you feel because they've been in your situation. They operate a social and support network for those widowed up to the age of 50. I have been impressed by what they do and the level of support that is offered so I'm sure they could be a rock to you during this time and beyond. And remember, after Christmas comes a New Year and a chance for us all to start again.

In the meantime you are in my thoughts and I wish you all the best that life can offer.

Dear Denise

My son died from cot death two months ago and I can't cope. I understand that older people die but how on earth am I supposed to deal with the death of my baby? It seems so wrong, so utterly unfair. I can't talk to anyone, I don't even have the words to express how I feel. I can't live my life knowing that my son has gone.

Dear X

The loss of anyone we love is a devastating blow, but I think that the loss of a child is particularly difficult to comprehend or come to terms with. I'm not going to insult you with empty words or phrases. We both know that life will never be the same and that you will never forget your baby. But that is not to say that you won't one day find contentment and be able to remember your first child with the love that he deserves as your first and very special baby. However, one can eventually find a way of living with loss and you will find a way through this. No one who reads your words could fail to understand what you have been through and what you have suffered and my heart goes out to you.

My first concern is whether you have had the opportunity to talk through your grief with someone. Is this something you feel you would like to do given the chance? If so, then the *Stillbirth and Neonatal Death Society* (020 7436 5881) would support you and you could talk to them about your baby and what he means – they would understand and listen. I completely understand that you feel so bereft at the moment. It is still very early days to be able to take in what has happened, but in time the grief you feel now will subside and only love for your son remain.

Be kind to yourself and listen to what your heart tells you that you need. Can you talk to your partner and share your grief? Are there friends or other family you can confide in? Sometimes people won't ask questions for fear of upsetting their loved one, but if you were to talk about the baby, remembering he was their baby too, wouldn't they reach out to you?

15

Your stories

*We had such hopes for our retirement,
for many happy years of travel and
enjoying our home together. We had
just over a year and then he was gone.
The principal thing I felt was anger,
fury at all the years of scrimping and
saving for nothing. For a while I
couldn't even enjoy being with our
children because they reminded me of
him. If I hadn't found a counsellor who
understood I don't know what I would
have done. Now I realize that I have to
do all those things we planned, not just
for myself but for him. You can't let a
dream die, you have to make an effort
even when it feels as though the heart
has gone out of it.*

Wendy

I realize now that you should be taught something about how to handle a death. We all sat around wondering what to do first. The doctor said to call an undertaker but we didn't know one. There were dozens in Yellow Pages but we didn't know which one would be the best. The one we picked was helpful but he kept asking what we wanted and no one knew. I wish there was a book you could get and just put by. If you did that you'd probably never need it but if you don't know what to do you just feel this terror that the whole thing is beyond you. My sister said if we didn't register the death in time we could go to prison, that's how much we knew. I'm wiser now but it was a savage way to get clued up. I hope it will be a long time before I have to do it again.

Liz

My husband died when we were on holiday. The people at the hospital were very nice but at times I didn't understand them. It was two days before my son got there and I must have cried my eyes out before then. I didn't often think about being widowed but if I did I thought I'd handle it all right. I hadn't realized how empty you feel and as though your arms and legs have been cut away. Everyone kept urging me to eat but food stuck in my throat. It was better when I got home. The doctor suggested I got in contact with Cruse and they helped me work through my grief. I only go to the cemetery occasionally now but I think about my husband every day. I think I always will even though I have a friend now, a nice man who lost his wife. The girls pull my leg about it and say they'll buy hats for the wedding but it's a big step to take.

Naomi

I used to wonder what I'd do when my parents died but that seemed such a long way off I just hoped I'd cope when the time came. I never gave a thought to losing anyone of my own age. When Dave died I couldn't come to terms with it. It wasn't that it was a terrible accident, it was that he was so young, such a one for a joke. What helped was seeing his mother be so brave about it. She wanted to do something to make sure he wouldn't be forgotten and so we have started to fundraise. We'll do something for kids and sport, I think, because he was always happiest with a ball at his feet.

At first I couldn't go out for a pint with the lads without welling up because he was always the loudest one there but I'm OK now. We can even remember some of his mad stunts and have a laugh. There'll never be anyone like him.

Tim

Part 5:
More Help
at Hand

In Chapters 16 and 17 of Part 5 we will look at what you can do to keep in good health after bereavement. You will find aids to relaxation such as visualization, meditation and breathing techniques that you might like to try. You will also find advice on diet and exercise and how to deal with worry. These are useful as strategies when perhaps everything feels too much, for low moments or when you need to spend some time by yourself, looking after yourself. As we have seen grieving can take a lot of our energy and there are many simple ways to stay healthy when life is stressful. Taking care of ourselves, in simple ways, can help to ground us. The last section of Part 5 is dedicated to resources, making it easier for you to find bereavement care and other help.

Taking steps to keep ourselves healthy is important at any time but is perhaps especially so when we are grieving. As we have seen, grieving can take a lot of our energy, perhaps most of all in the early days when our bodies might have gone into shock and we were likely to feel disorientated, fidgety and perhaps prone to clumsiness. Looking after ourselves, in simple ways, can help to ground us. When we are in mourning for someone special who we loved deeply, we might not eat very much and possibly we can expect to have disturbed or difficult sleep patterns. Gradually over time, these usually sort themselves out and our appetite returns and we begin to sleep better, but there are things that we can do to help. Taking steps to relax and de-stress our bodies is a fundamental aid to healing.

16

Helping you relax

Relaxation techniques are easy to learn and can be a real comfort when we are grieving. You might wonder 'Why do I need to relax – surely it's better if I keep busy?' While it is good to be busy at times, and it can help to do small tasks – it can make us feel in control and that we have order in our lives – it is also important to stop sometimes and rest and recharge our batteries. Practising relaxation techniques can help with anxiety and depression. People relax in many different ways and it is important that you find ways that work for you.

Relaxation techniques

Relaxation techniques include the practice of visualization and meditation and paying attention to our thoughts and our breathing. Yoga, other forms of exercise and massage can also help us to relax. Anything that relaxes us and allows us to switch off is a relaxation technique that we can adopt to improve our feeling of well-being. Ways of relaxing encourage us to control our minds (in favour of more positive thoughts) and enjoy our bodies. We learn how to be sensuous and take pleasure in ourselves, with others, and our environment. We learn to take time in what we do and build tranquillity and calmness into our lives.

Meditation

In the West, meditation is commonly used as a means of relaxation and its aim is to still the mind and to develop a serene detachment from life's problems to help people cope with problems more effectively. Meditation techniques have been adapted and simplified for this purpose.

However, it isn't really necessary to place meditation in the context of its ancient traditions when we use the basics of meditation to build self-awareness, release tension and still the mind. During meditation breathing is conscious rather than automatic. Breathing takes place through the nostrils and we breath slowly and deeply. Try the following exercises to get you started and, if you are interested, you could join a local meditation group or buy a book or DVD on meditation. You will find that there is a lot of crossover between meditation, visualization and relaxation exercises. All relaxation techniques concentrate on the breath and focus on visualized images, objects or sounds. Try to make sure that you carry out relaxation exercises in quiet, warm, comfortable surroundings where you are unlikely to be disturbed. Wear loose comfortable clothing and to avoid discomfort sit in a position that you find comfortable.

A basic meditation exercise

Try to empty your mind of any distractions by focusing on a chosen image or object. This might be something like a lighted candle, a vase of flowers or a picture (placed in front of you), or you might like to close your eyes and concentrate on a soothing or uplifting mental image. Alternatively, try repeating a word, phrase or sound over and over again. Keep it simple. Try using the word 'calm' as you take a deep inhalation and the word 'serenity' as you exhale. After 10 to 20 minutes slowly return to everyday life and enjoy the relaxing effects of the exercise.

Attention to breathing

By focusing on our breathing we can become more aware of our levels of stress. For instance, do you know if you normally breathe deeply or shallowly, fast or slow? When we breathe correctly it comes from the diaphragm, shallow breath comes from the chest. To test yourself, lie down on the floor and try to relax – feel the tensions in your body and then let them drop away, let your body flop. Next, place your hands over your abdomen and take a few long, slow, deep breaths and note what happens. We often think that our abdomen goes in when we inhale when in fact the opposite is true – it should raise slightly and flatten as we exhale. You will feel benefits from simply making sure you are breathing in a way that ensures that you are taking in and expelling adequate levels of oxygen and carbon dioxide. When our breathing is fast and shallow we expel too much carbon dioxide, which can make us light headed and dizzy and prone to anxiety attacks.

Yoga, meditation, visualization and body desensitization exercises all focus on effective breathing. These are ways to relax that are useful when your body might be tense and stressed with grief. You might have become tensed without even noticing it – perhaps you feel strung out and weepy and still unable to settle at times. You are likely to have suffered mood swings. When we are traumatized we hold our bodies rigidly and this can cause aches and pains and stiffness in places like the shoulders and neck. Perhaps, since the death of your loved one, you have had to take on more responsibilities and worries and you are overstretched mentally and physically. If this is the case, it is important that you find ways to unwind and de-stress.

If you do try meditation or visualization it might feel strange because you aren't used to it. At first, you are likely to find it hard to sustain concentration for any length of time and all sorts of random thoughts and images might flit through your mind. It is important that you accept these and avoid trying to control or attach yourself to them – just be aware of them as they come and go and return your attention to the focus of the exercise and if you persevere your concentration will improve. Take it slowly, a few minutes at a time, and build up to longer periods.

Simple stretching yogic exercises will help with body tenseness. Think of animals, like cats, and how they stretch their bodies regularly and how relaxed and chilled out they normally are. Slow and deep breathing is the basis for all relaxation techniques so try to get into the habit of breathing in this way. If you do you will have more energy. Taking fresh air into our lungs is also vital to good health and, when weather permits, we can exercise outside for added benefits.

Breathing exercises

These exercises will relax you and make you more aware of your body and any tensions you hold.

Letting go of tension through the breath

Begin by sitting comfortably in a chair or on the floor. Close your eyes. Rest your hands on your thighs or on the arms of the chair. As you rest, notice the sensations in your body as they are in the moment. You might become aware of the feel of the shoes on your feet or notice the sensations in your hands or your shoulders or neck. Breathe easily and deeply and become aware of the sensations as you breathe, noticing the differences when you breathe in and fill your lungs, and then notice the sense of release as you breathe out. Simply concentrate on your breath for five to ten minutes. Some people find it helpful to count as you breathe in and out; try using a count of four for each.

A simple yogic breathing exercise

Stand straight, feet hip width apart, arms by your side and palms facing inwards. Take a slow, deep breath through the nostrils to fill your lungs and hold the breath while you perform the rest of the exercise.

Raise your arms to shoulder level keeping palms in the same position. In a continuous movement and keeping your elbows straight, bring the palms of your hands together to meet over your head. To complete the exercise, turn your palms outward and exhale through the mouth while you bring your arms down slowly to your sides to the original position. Empty the lungs by contracting the muscles in the lung area as you continue to exhale.

A deep muscle relaxation exercise

Wearing loose comfortable clothes, lie on the floor on a thick large towel or mat (or on a firm mattress), with your legs straight and arms by your side. Let yourself get comfortable. Close your eyes and relax. Try to surrender yourself to the experience and breathe naturally and easily.

You are going to work through your body, first tensing then relaxing the various parts, beginning with the toes and feet and working upwards, finishing with the top of your head. Move in this order: toes to feet, feet to calves, calves to thighs, thighs to buttocks, buttocks to abdomen, abdomen to chest and back, chest and back to hands, hands to arms, arms to shoulder and neck, shoulder and neck to the muscles of the face, face to scalp and top of the head.

Breathe in deeply as you tense each muscle area, hold the breath while the muscles are tense (for five seconds) then exhale as you let go and relax. On each exhalation notice a feeling of growing relaxation and well-being flowing through the area as you work your way up towards the top of your head.

On completion, breathe naturally and place awareness in how relaxed and at peace you feel.

Notice your breathing; on each exhalation feel yourself becoming increasingly relaxed and at ease. Yawning is common as tension is released from the body.

Simple meditative 'practise anywhere' relaxation exercise

Think of a mental image or sound that is relaxing for you and that you can use as a tool to switch off. This might be words like 'calm' or 'relax' or 'Om' (a word commonly used as a sound in meditation mantras), or a relaxing still image such as a beautiful view from a window or a stretch of beach. In fact it can be anything that you associate with peace and tranquillity.

Sit in a comfortable position (whether this is at home or on a train journey or on a park bench), and breathe slowly and smoothly and imagine your body becoming heavier and more relaxed. Now, starting at your feet, move up through your body to the top of your head, scanning for any areas of tension and relaxing any tension you find. When your body is heavy and relaxed, turn your attention on your breathing once again.

Breathing easily and naturally, breathe in

through your nose and fill your lungs to full capacity; as you breathe out focus on your chosen mental image or sound and breathe naturally as you do this. Repeat this pattern of breathing in fully through your nose and out through your nose, then focus on your chosen relaxation device as you breathe naturally. Continue this pattern until you feel calm, relaxed and revived. Sit quietly for a few more minutes enjoying the feelings of relaxation.

Visualization

To give you an example of what visualization is and how it can help, repeat an exercise given in Part 3, Chapter 11 (page 194). Spend a few moments thinking about a place you have visited that you enjoyed – choose somewhere where you felt really happy and relaxed. It might be a visit to the seaside with your children (or as a child yourself), a mountain walk with a loved one or sitting at a pavement café by yourself watching the world go by on a hot summer's day. When you have chosen what you are going to think about, sit somewhere comfortable and begin with breathing slowly and deeply, then picture yourself in that place, and picture it in detail. Think of the sights, smells, sounds, tastes and sensations – use all of your senses. If you are at the seaside you might hear the seagulls and children's laughter, perhaps you can feel the grittiness of the sand between your toes, see the blueness of the sea and sky, and smell or taste the saltiness of the ocean. When this exercise comes to a natural end, be aware of how relaxed and refreshed you feel.

The following is an effective visualization exercises for the bereaved.

Visualization exercise to address 'unfinished business'

We sometimes have dreams about the person we cared about after they died. In these dreams they might be healthy, happy and at peace. We might receive messages of love or assurance and be comforted. We might have conversations with them, when we are given the opportunity to say things we wished we had said to them when they were alive. Dreams like these can be reassuring but we then awake to the reality that the person has died and we are likely to feel distraught once more. However, we can take dream images like these and visualize them at will to help us resolve issues we feel uneasy about.

Sit in a comfortable position, and let bodily tensions drop away. Close your eyes and focus on your breathing; breathe slowly and deeply. When you feel ready, think of the deceased and let yourself feel filled with love for them. Picture them, as you would want them to be, perhaps care and worry free. Imagine a white light surrounding you as the love you feel for the person intensifies; then imagine the light reaching out and enveloping them too. Feel love emanating from the person back to you. Think of the light as spiritual protection, protecting and soothing both of you.

Now picture yourself talking to them about any unresolved issues you believe there might be left between you. Try to see them as understanding and responsive in return. Say what you need to say to them. Imagine what they say to you in return. When you feel ready to finish, thank your loved one and tell them what you wish for them and see them as being at peace with themselves and with you. As they go, visualize them as still surrounded by the white light. Feel the white light separate and also surround you. Spend a few more minutes sitting in the light. Let yourself be filled with the sense of spiritual love and protection. Open your eyes and give yourself a moment to come out of the exercise.

Aids to sleep

Sleep can be disturbed for some time after bereavement. There are, however, many ways to help re-establish a restful sleeping pattern. It is important that the sleep environment is a restful one. Ask yourself: 'Is my bedroom currently an invigorating vibrant place to be?' or 'Is it a serene and peaceful room?' If it is bright red, has a computer in one corner and a television facing the bed, then it is unlikely to invite restful sleep. Ideally a bedroom should be decorated in serene, soft pastel colours and be uncluttered. It needs to be restful on the eye, with soft subdued lighting. Remember your bedroom is a place to sleep, relax and rest and isn't an office, so try to avoid having computers or other work related articles in your bedroom that might remind you subliminally of work. Televisions can also be intrusive – you might think that it is relaxing to watch television in bed but it is a stimulating activity best enjoyed in another room that has no associations with sleep.

Try to avoid stimulants such as tea and coffee, and eating heavy meals close to bedtime if you are having trouble sleeping . Also if you can, avoid excitement – no action films or reading thrillers. You might think that sex can be classed as stimulating and exciting and that it follows that having sex with your partner at bedtime might also keep you awake but this isn't so. Sex can deeply relax the body and is therefore likely to help you fall into a deep slumber.

It helps to develop a bedtime routine that gets your mind and body prepared for sleep. Try switching the television or computer off a couple of hours (and a minimum of one hour) before bedtime. Listen to some soothing music, have a warm bath and cup of hot milk. It also helps to establish a sleep routine – try going to bed around the same time every night to help you establish sleep patterns. If you wake in the middle of the night, it won't help to toss and turn and worry about lack of sleep. Instead, try getting up and doing something mundane like washing the kitchen floor, mend something or you could read something boring. (It is said that when medical students can't sleep, they read medical tomes like *Grey's Anatomy*.)

If you can't sleep you could try the deep muscle relaxing exercise on page 287 that systematically and deeply relaxes all the different muscle groups in the body by first tensing and then relaxing the muscles. Or you might like to try the following:

Sleep inducing exercise

Choose a point on the ceiling to focus on (for example, a light fitting), then from your peripheral vision choose an article in the room (perhaps a curtain or a picture on the wall) to add to the main object of your focus. Then keep adding items from your peripheral vision from the room to the main object (the light fitting) as before. The combination of concentrating on the additions and looking up at the central point will tire your eyes and you will become sleepy.

Mental task

Try something mentally tiring, take a random letter of the alphabet and think of all the films, books or songs beginning with that letter, or try to remember the names of everyone who was in your class at school, or list all the jobs you have had.

Simple self-hypnosis technique

Try some self-hypnosis to help you get to sleep. The bedroom should be warm but well ventilated. Make yourself comfortable in your bed and if you are lying on your side then perhaps arrange your pillow at an angle so that your neck is supported. Breathing deeply and slowly, imagine your mind and body getting heavier and heavier. Let all tensions go. Tell yourself you feel so, so, relaxed... Say in your mind 'I can feel myself drifting further and further and deeper and deeper into restful sleep.' Believe this is happening. You are aware of your mind losing focus and that you are entering into ever deeper layers of relaxation. Tell yourself that you are going into deep, care free sleep and let thoughts and concerns drift away as you are caressed by soft, warm feelings of contentment.

Try not to worry too much if you are losing sleep. When we sleep badly we often make the situation tenser by worrying about it. Lack of sleep over a long time can have an effect on our health but most of us sleep badly at times and people don't die from lack of sleep. It is a good idea to nap during the day when we are recently bereaved and not sleeping well, but later it isn't such a good idea since we need to let our bodies get tired. Keep routines in preparation for sleep and you should notice improvements.

Maintaining a healthy diet

Try to eat as well as you can. Even though it might be difficult for you to even think about food at times, it is important to your general well-being. Resorting to convenience foods would be understandable, but it is best, when you can, to avoid pre-packed and junk foods and to choose wholesome, nutritional food. Eating a wholesome diet containing a balance of protein, carbohydrates, pulses and fruit and vegetables will ensure you are getting all the nutrients your body needs to help you through this stressful time.

Eat as regularly as you can – if you can't face large meals then why not try eating small meals every few hours'? Eating regularly helps to keep your blood sugar levels on an even keel. Scientific evidence tells us that if our blood sugars dip too low – usually through hunger – we are more prone to mood swings and depression. High carbohydrate and sugar snacks, like chocolate bars, give us a rush of energy that then dips after a short time leaving us more tired than before.

Drink alcohol in moderation only and try reducing your caffeine intake in coffee, tea and cola drinks – perhaps you could try alternatives like herb or fruit teas, decaffeinated tea or coffee or dandelion coffee.

Our blood sugar levels also affect our concentration and can make us more prone to anxiety attacks. In connection with eating habits, the mental health organization *MIND*, recommends that those suffering from anxiety attacks:

- Eat every few hours to keep blood sugar levels even.

- Eat a balanced diet rich in nutrients.

- Avoid high sugar content foods that cause sugar levels to rise suddenly then dip soon afterwards.

- Reduce the intake of stimulants like tea, coffee and alcohol.

Physical exercise

Take regular physical exercise – try to find something you enjoy doing. Try joining a gym or taking a yoga class, brisk walking or cycling. Don't forget that gardening and housework is exercise too. If you are older contact your local *Socials Services* or *Age Concern* to find out about exercise classes tailored to the needs of your age group. When we exercise, chemicals called endorphins are released in our brain and other parts of our bodies and the result is we feel more positive. Also exercise gets the blood flowing around our bodies, which is good for our circulation and energy levels.

17

Positive thinking

Try to be positive in your thoughts and learn to do things that make you feel good.

- Follow the saying 'Don't sweat the small stuff' – life is too short. Make a relaxed attitude to life a habit and if something is a real worry, then vow to do something about it.

- Think of life as something to be enjoyed.

- Take regular exercise in a form that lifts your spirits.

- Put half an hour aside each day to practise relaxation techniques like meditation, visualization or relaxation exercises.

- Think of yourself as worth looking after – take regular breaks, give yourself treats and pamper yourself.

- Make time for friends and family and have regular get-togethers.

- Set yourself realistic challenges and don't worry about failing (we all fail at times). Better still reframe 'failing' as 'I tried but it wasn't for me'.

- Build in time to play – laughter, fun, spend time with children or young people.

Don't get dragged down by worry

Most of us spend a lot of time worrying about problem scenarios (and what imaginations we have!). It can cause us to be distracted and fractious in the day and keep us awake at night. Worrying can make it hard to relax. Sometimes the worry is real but usually it is either irrational or exaggerated in our minds. We simply get things out of proportion. It is understandable to behave this way after bereavement but we don't do ourselves any favours by making a habit of it. If we do worry, it makes sense to identify the problems and do something about them. It will help if we:

Identify the problem Ask yourself 'What am I worried about?' Sometimes we think it is one thing and it might be another. For instance, you might be worried about a situation at work where you feel you are not coping with your workload. You might be telling yourself, as a worse case scenario, that if you talk to your manager about how you are feeling then you will lose your job. (Often we make huge catastrophic leaps in our thinking.) Although this feels very real to you, it might be that this worry is triggered by a deeper worry about coping and providing for your family (for instance, in relation to bereavement following the death of your spouse). If this is the case then try to remind yourself to deal with life step by step and not to predict too far into the future.

Build stepping stones to solve the problem Once you have identified the nature of your worries you can take steps, however small, to solve the problem. This might involve talking to someone, making arrangements or coming to a decision, and when you begin the process it will feel better.

Scale the problem To gauge how much the problem is affecting your life, on a scale of one to ten, score how important your worry actually is, taking one as not very important and ten as crucial to your happiness and well-being. If the score is low, you will feel reassured and might question why you have been so worried and if the problem scores highly on both counts then make up your mind to do something about it.

Reality test the situation Be realistic. You might need to reality test the situation. Ask yourself questions such as: 'What evidence is there that this is so?' 'Is it my responsibility?' 'Is the problem helped by my worrying about it?' 'Is my avoidance giving the problem more power over me than needs be?' and 'Am I a victim of my own or other people's "musts", "shoulds" and "oughts"?'

If you are telling yourself that you won't be able to cope about some imagined situation then ask yourself how likely it is to happen. What is the evidence that this could happen? For instance, in the above situation, has there been a case when, after talking to a manager about their workload, a person was sacked? Suppose you worry that the death of your partner means that your children's lives are ruined forever by their father's death. To reassure yourself, look at the experiences of other families whose children suffered a similar loss and how they got through it, and think of the ways in which your children have shown their ability to bounce back after difficulties. Reassure yourself that children do recover from the loss of someone they loved dearly. Often our worries are projected onto other people, when we imagine their responses. Try to do something about what it is actually possible to change and let go of the rest.

Compartmentalize your worry Worrying can become a habit. You could try giving yourself a half hour a day to worry, at the end of which put the worries aside. It might feel ludicrous to sit and worry at will and you might not even be able to do it, but put the worries aside anyway. Sit and think about your problems and then when the half hour is up, say to yourself that's enough. It can add a little light heartedness to problem solving.

Give the worry away Imagine yourself as a wise sage – what advice would you give to the problem? Or imagine it is a loved friend who has the problem. What would you say to them?

Be determined to enjoy life Be good to yourself, give yourself treats, things to look forward to that give you pleasure and keep active. It is harder to be depressed and to worry when we are busy and our minds and bodies are occupied.

Regeneration

As we have seen, a big part of getting over the death of a loved one is the acceptance that they have gone from our physical lives. Through the healing powers of time we begin to understand that we haven't totally lost the person because we keep them in our hearts and in the memories we have of all the times we spent together. If we love the deceased, and choose to, we can take the person into our consciousness as part of ourselves and perhaps the emphasis changes from 'I'll never get over that I've lost them' to 'I'm glad that I knew them and that they were, and still are, part of my life and I'll never forget them.'

Gradually our interest and enjoyment of the outer world returns and we are able to invest our love and attentions in other interests and people. We find reasons to carry on. We might find love again in the form of a partnership and if we do, we realize that the relationship and the love we share is not a substitute or a replacement of the person who died but is unique in itself; just as when we have a second child, we don't love the first child any less and yet we have love in our hearts for the other child as well.

There comes a time when once again we can

feel hopeful. Perhaps bonds have been strengthened with those who have helped us through our grieving and we might have become more aware of what is important to us in our lives, of what we value and cherish. Life might have taken on a new immediacy and we become determined to live life to the full and appreciate those around us. You might have decided to become more adventurous and you may be more acutely aware of your strengths and capabilities. There have been lessons to learn – hard earned, but you have learnt. Try listing what you are grateful for in your life before you go to bed each night. Is the glass half full or half empty? All of us have some elements in our lives we can be grateful for (that's not to say your life is all rosy and there are no problems or difficulties, but that there are probably some wonderful parts too).

It makes sense to look at the whole picture as it can:

- Lift our spirits.

- Make us more self-aware and feel good about ourselves and our lives.

- Give us an appreciation of people close to us.

- Make us more optimistic.

- Make us more adventurous.

- Make us determined to make the most of the time we have left to live.

- Give us an awareness of what we value in life.

- Make us live in the here and now.

- Make us trust in the restorative quality and cycles of life.

18

Books and support networks

Books

Funerals and burial

Funerals without God – J. W. Willson, British
Humanist Association, 1989.
Green Burial: the DIY Guide to Law and Practice –
J. B. Bradfield, Natural Death Centre, 1994.
What to Do when Somebody Dies – Which Books,
Consumer Association, 1991.

Bereavement

Death – The Final Stage of Growth – Elizabeth
Kubler-Ross, Englewood Cliffs, 1975.
Thoughts of Power and Love – Susan Jeffers,
Coronet, 1997.
You'll Get Over It! – Virginia Ironside, Hamish
Hamilton, 1996.

Practical help

The Natural Death Handbook – ed. Nicholas
Albery, The Natural Death Centre, 1998.
What to Do when Somebody Dies – Which Books,
Consumers Association, 1991.
What to Do after a Death in England and Wales –
Benefit Agency Communications.

Wills and Probate – Which Books, 1995.
The Which Guide to Giving and Inheriting –
J. Lowe, 1994.

Self-help and relaxation

Teach Yourself Healthy Eating – W. Doyle, Hodder
Education, 1994.
The Relaxation and Stress Reduction Workbook –
M. Davis, E. Robbins Eshelman and M. McKay,
Harbinger Publications, 2000.
Teach Yourself Meditation – N. Ozaniec, Hodder
Education, 2006.
Teach Yourself Relaxation – Richard Craze,
Hodder Education, 2003.

Support networks

There are many resources relating to bereavement, for example, bereavement care agencies that offer counselling and support, benefit agencies and pension related organizations. None of us needs to feel ill-informed or unsupported through difficult times. You need to reach out and check your local and national agencies to access support and advice. The internet is an invaluable source of information, offering a wealth of resources. All you need to do is type in a short description of what you are looking for, for instance, 'bereavement care', into a search engine like Google, Lycos, or Yahoo and see where it takes you. Sites will signpost you to other related helpful sites.

Army Widows Association
c/o AIASC Building 43, Trenchard Lines, Upavon Wiltshire SN9 6BE
Tel: 01980 615558
website: **www.armywidows.org.uk**

A bereavement support group offering comfort, support and friendship to the widows, widowers and dependants of army personnel who die in service. The Army Widows Association aims to address some of the difficulties encountered after the death.

The Child Bereavement Trust

Aston House, High Street, West Wycombe
Buckinghamshire HP14 3AG
Tel: 01494 446648
Helpline: 0845 357 1000
email: enquiries@childbereavement.org.uk
website: **www.childbereavement.org.uk**

Objects: To encourage the understanding of the needs of grieving families and promote good practice in the quality of care and support offered to them. To offer support and training to professionals who care for bereaved families in whatever capacity.

Activities: Provides specialist training in bereavement counselling skills for healthcare professionals, teachers, voluntary sector workers and anyone who offers professional care to families when a baby or child dies. Runs seminars, workshops and conferences. Provides resources for families.

Child Death Helpline

Great Ormond Street Hospital for Children
Great Ormond Street
London WC1N 3JH
Tel: 020 7813 8551
Helpline: 0800 282982 (Mon–Fri 10.00 a.m.–1.00
p.m. and Wed 1.00 p.m.–5 p.m. Every evening
7 p.m.–10 p.m.)
Fax: 020 7813 8516
email: contact@childdeathhelpline.org
website: **www.childdeathhelpline.org.uk**

Objects: To provide a quality freephone service to
all those affected by the death of a child, offering
a confidential, safe and supportive environment
within which a caller can talk openly about their
child's life and death.

Activities: A lifetime emotional support service
to anyone affected by the death of a child of any
age (from miscarriage to adult children), under
any circumstances, however long ago. Callers
often find it comforting to talk and describe the
worries and emotions that unexpectedly
overwhelm them or return after many years.

The Compassionate Friends
53 North Street
Bristol BS3 1EN
Tel: 0117 966 5202
Helpline: 0845 123 2304 (Mon–Sun
10 a.m.–4.30 p.m. and 6.30 p.m.–10 p.m.)
Fax: 0117 914 4368
email: info@tcf.org.uk
website: **www.tcf.org.uk**

Objects: Support and friendship for bereaved parents and their families by those who are similarly bereaved.
Activities: Befriending, support and understanding are offered through a national telephone helpline; local telephone support; visits to the family; personal and group support; quarterly newsletters; leaflets and articles; books and booklets; annual weekend gathering; postal library.

Cruse Bereavement Care
126 Sheen Road, Richmond upon Thames
Surrey TW9 1UR
Tel: 020 8939 9530
Helpline: 0870 167 1677; Fax: 020 8940 7636
email: info@crusebereavementcare.org.uk
website: **www.crusebereavementcare.org.uk**

Objects: Cruse Bereavement Care is the UK's largest and only national organization that helps and supports anyone who has been bereaved by death. Since 1959 Cruse has been providing advice, bereavement support and information on practical matters for bereaved people entirely free of charge. Support is delivered through a network of 150 branches throughout England, Wales and Northern Ireland. Cruse also offers training, support, information and publications to those working to care for bereaved people. Cruse aims to increase public awareness of the needs of bereaved people through education and information services.

Edward's Trust
43a Calthorpe Road, Edgbaston
Birmingham B15 1TS
Tel: 0121 237 5656
Fax: 0121 237 5657
email: admin@edwardstrust.fsbusiness.co.uk
website: **www.edwardstrust.org.uk**

Objects: To promote the relief of children and families who have suffered the death of a child from conception onwards and of children who have suffered the death of a parent, primary carer or sibling.

Activities: Meeting accommodation needs for families while their child is being treated in Birmingham. Supporting the Sunrise West Midlands Child Bereavement Centre (Tel: 0121 454 1705) for families. All services are free to families who have a sick child or who have lost a child from whatever cause.

Foundation for the Study of Infant Deaths (Cot Death Research and Support)
Artillery House, 11–19 Artillery Row
London SW1P 1RT
Tel: 0870 787 0855
Helpline: 0870 787 0554 (24 hours)
Fax: 0870 787 0725
email: fsid@sids.org.uk
website: **www.sids.org.uk/fsid**

Objects: To promote and sponsor research into the cause and prevention of sudden and unexpected deaths and into infant health; to support and counsel bereaved parents; to be a centre for information and exchange of knowledge in the UK and abroad.

Activities: Offers support to bereaved families through its 24-hour helpline and local befrienders. Sponsors research, publishes material on research findings, advises on preventing death and promoting health.

Gingerbread
307 Borough High Street
London SE1 IJH
Tel: 0207 403 9500
Freephone: 0800 018 4318
Fax: 0207 403 9533
email: office@gingerbread.org.uk
membership@gingerbread.org.uk
advice@gingerbread.org.uk
website: **www.gingerbread.org.uk**

Gingerbread is an organization for lone parent families. It is the leading and largest charity providing help for 1.8 million lone parents and their children throughout England and Wales. It provides advice and an expert and confidential freephone service dealing with a varied range of queries, for example, on benefits, legal matters, housing and counselling. It offers help to counter the effects of childhood poverty by organizing holidays, discount vouchers, outings and events to ensure that children are not excluded from activities and opportunities.

MIND

The National Association for Mental Health,
Granta House, 15–19 Broadway
Stratford, London E15 4BQ
Tel: 020 8519 2122
website: **www.mind.org.uk**

MIND is a leading mental health charity with local associations in 200 locations throughout England and Wales. MIND produces information booklets and leaflets on subjects like coping with anxiety attacks and nutrition and mental health.

Rainbow Centre for Children Affected by Life-Threatening Illnesses or Bereavement

(formerly Rainbow Centre for Children with Cancer and Life-Threatening Illness)
27 Lilymead Avenue
Bristol BS4 2BY
Tel: 0117 985 3343
Fax 0117 985 3353
email: contact@rainbowcentre.fsnet.co.uk
website: **www.rainbowcentre.org.uk**

Objects: The support of children and their families experiencing cancer and other life-threatening illnesses or bereavement, using counselling and complementary therapies.

Activities: Provides emotional and psychological support for each family member and the family as a unit during the period of crisis: counsellors and therapists work with clients at the Centre, in their own homes and sometimes in hospital. Offers: counselling art therapy; relaxation and visualization techniques; massage; advice on diet; and introductions to other helpful therapies.

Stillbirth and Neonatal Death Society (SANDS)

28 Portland Place
London W1B 1LY
Tel: 020 7436 7940 (admin & publications)
Helpline: 020 7436 5881 (Mon–Fri 10 a.m. – 3 p.m.)
Fax: 020 7436 3715
email: support@uk-sands.org
website: **www.uk-sands.org**

Objects: SANDS provides support for bereaved parents and their families when their baby dies at or soon after birth.

Activities: The key elements of that support are: national telephone helpline service; UK-wide network of local self-help groups run by and for bereaved parents; information and publications for bereaved parents and healthcare professionals.

Soldiers, Sailors, Airmen and Families Association (SSAFA) Forces Help

SSAFA,
19 Queen Elizabeth St.
London
SE1 2LP
Tel: Central Office - 0207 4038783
General enquires: 0845 1300 975
email: **info@ssafa.org.uk**
website: www.ssafa.org.uk/

The SSAFA is a civilian charity founded in 1885 to support the families of Service personnel. The work of the association is governed by its Council, under the terms of a Royal Charter. Those eligible for assistance from SSAFA Forces Help are: Service personnel, wives, families, widows and other dependents of all ranks of all branches of Land, Sea and Air Forces of the Crown, whether serving or formerly serving, and, in certain cases UK based Civilians (UKBCs) and their families. SSAFA have a welfare department and a bereavement and funeral department.

Survivors of Bereavement by Suicide (SOBS)
14–18 West Bar Green
Sheffield S1 2DA
Tel: 01482 610728
Helpline: 0870 241 3337 (seven days a week
9 a.m.–9 p.m.)
For details of a local counselling service,
call 01779 470163
Fax: 01482 210287
email: sobs.admin@care4free.net
website: **www.uk-sobs.org.uk**

Objects: To meet the needs and break the isolation of those bereaved by the suicide of a close relative or friend and to promote mental health, well-being, confidence, self-esteem and coping strategies to aid recovery.
Activities: National helpline, support groups in various locations, support days, retreats, training (both volunteer and professional), quarterly newsletters.

Winston's Wish (WW)
Clara Burgess Centre
Bayshill Road, Cheltenham
Glos. GL50 3AW
Tel: 01242 515157
Helpline: 0845 203 0405 (Mon–Fri 9.30 a.m.–5 p.m.)
Fax: 01242 546187
email: info@winstonswish.org.uk
website: **www.winstonswish.org.uk**

Objects: Winston's Wish is an award winning charity, which supports bereaved children and young people following the death of a parent or sibling.

Activities: Provides a family line (0845 2030 405) and a range of practical resources and publications for bereaved children and young people and the adults working with them. it also provides an interactive website for young people and training and consultancy services.

Other useful contacts

Age Concern
Astral House
1268 London Road
London SW16 4ER
Helpline: 0800 009966 (Mon–Sun 8 a.m.–7 p.m.)
General enquiries: 020 8765 7200
email: ace@ace.org.uk
website: **www.ageconcern.org.uk**

**Association for British Counselling and
Psychotherapy (BACP)**
Tel: 0870 443 5252

The British Humanist Association (BHA)
Tel: 020 7079 3580

Carers UK
Tel: 020 7490 8818
email: info@carersuk.org
website: **www.carersuk.org**

Consumer Credit Counselling Service
Freephone: 0800 138 1111
email: contactus@cccs.co.uk
website: **www.cccs.co.uk**

Department for Work and Pensions
Tel: 020 7712 2171 (Mon–Fri 9 a.m.–5 p.m)
website: **www.dwp.gov.uk**
Pays benefits including Bereavement Allowance, Bereaved Parents Benefit and State Retirement Pensions.

Drugline (for those affected by drug use either directly or indirectly)
Tel: 020 8692 4975

The Family Contact Line
Tel: 0161 941 4011 (10 a.m.–10 p.m.)

Help the Aged
207–221 Pentonville Road
London N1 9UZ
Tel: 020 7278 1114
Helpline: 0808 800 6565
Fax: 020 7278 1116
email: info@helptheaged.org.uk
website: **www.helptheaged.org.uk**

Inland Revenue
(see local telephone directory)
website: **www.hmrc.gov.uk**

Lesbian and Gay Bereavement Project
Tel: 020 7403 5969

Macmillan Cancer Relief
Tel: 0808 808 2020

National AIDS Helpline
Tel (Freephone): 0800 567 123

National Association of Funeral Directors
Tel: 0121 711 1343

National Association of Widows
48 Queens Road
Coventry CV1 3EH
Tel: 0845 838 2261
Fax: 0845 838 2261
email: info@nawidows.org.uk
website: **www.nawidows.org.uk**

Provides information and support to all widows.
There are local branches and the national
organization arranges regular meetings and
conferences. It publishes a survival guide for
widows and a number of pamphlets.

National Council for the Divorced and Separated

51 Jubilee Way
Necton
Swaffham
PE37 8LZ
Tel: 07041 478 120
website: **www.ncds.org.uk/cms**

Membership of the NCDS is available to all divorced, separated and widowed people – the organization specializes in helping you start a new social life.

The National Society of Allied and Independent Funeral Directors (SAIF)

Tel: 0845 230 6777

The Natural Death Centre

6 Blackstock Mews
Blackstock Road
London N4 2BT
Tel: 0871 288 2098
Fax: 020 7354 3831
website: **www.naturaldeath.org.uk**

The Natural Death Centre is a charity that aims to improve the quality of dying by encouraging the discussion of death and dying and by helping people to prepare for their death emotionally and in practical ways. It campaigns for more support for people wishing to die at home. The organization is also a resource and referral centre for people seeking, for example, counsellors or funeral directors who will conduct particular types of funerals. It can also give information and advice on how to arrange a funeral without a funeral director, burials on private land and alternatives to traditional coffins.

No Panic (support for sufferers of panic attacks)
Tel: 01952 590545

Parentline
Tel: 0808 800 2222 – calls taken 24 hours a day, 7 days a week.

The Samaritans
Tel: 0845 790 9090
website: **www.samaritans.org.uk**

The Samaritans provides emotional support 24 hours a day, 7 days a week for everyone.

The Widowed and Young Foundation
Tel: 0870 011 3450

War Widows Association of Great Britain
Tel: 0870 2411 305
email: info@warwidowsassociation.org.uk
website: **www.warwidowsassociation.org.uk**

Good luck

We hope this book has helped and that the future will be happier and less frightening than you may at present fear. It comes with the sympathy and best wishes of everyone at *This Morning*.